Fast Track to Heaven

Fast Track to Heaven

Wit and Wisdom for LDS Women

LYNN C. JAYNES

Covenant Communications, Inc.

Covenant

Cover illustration by Eldon Doty © Photodisc Green/Getty Images, Inc.

Cover design copyrighted 2005 by Covenant Communications, Inc.

Published by Covenant Communications, Inc.
American Fork, Utah

Printed in the United States of America
First Printing: March 2005

11 10 09 08 07 06 05   10 9 8 7 6 5 4 3 2 1

ISBN 1-59156-752-1

for
my wonderful family

Table of Contents

Season III: As Sisters in Zion, We'll All Whine Together

Season IV: The Simmering Pot

Introduction

Readers, before we take ourselves too seriously, perhaps I should get something off my chest. (Why do people use that expression, "off my chest"? Frankly, we women with very little *on* our chests would like to keep whatever we have. But I digress . . .) This book is intended to help women feel better about themselves. Most of you are stronger than I am; who am I that I have any special gift to comfort you? Your struggles are huge, your tasks are monumental, your lives are complicated—and you handle it all with organization and efficiency and gentleness and nerves of steel. If this last part accurately describes you, then you are also in denial. Wake up, honey. At the very least, when you read this book, maybe you'll be able to say, "I may not do everything well but compared to her I'm not doing too badly, either."

This book could also be a parenting manual. It's just not a very good parenting manual. I personally wouldn't recommend it to anyone for that purpose. Everyone raises children differently, and even psychologists and family counselors can't agree on the best method. On the other hand, if you'd like to smile occasionally, despite your otherwise stressful world, while you read a poor parenting manual, then be my guest.

This book was also intended to be a spiritual guidebook. It just didn't turn out to be a really good spiritual guidebook. It's perhaps a bit zippy for such a serious subject, and perhaps a person as flawed as I am has no business in the spiritual arena anyway. However, if you can look past the times I was a little confused, a little lacking in water-walking faith, a little lacking in the Spirit—a little lacking in many, many things—and can simply appreciate the struggle, then read on.

The truth of it is, this book should just probably be for perspective. It's like driving down the street once the sun has gone down, and if you peer into the little homes with the curtains drawn back, you can glimpse into someone else's world, at someone else's kitchen table and chairs, someone else's family portraits, someone else's afghan thrown over the couch, and just for a tiny minute you can imagine what their lives might be like. This book is like one of those windows with the curtains drawn back, full of homely vignettes. When you're done peering in my window you might recognize that your own goofy life is really fairly sane. You might recognize that behind every façade in the neighborhood lives a woman who doesn't quite have it all together, who is screwing up pretty much on a daily basis, and who is really more into damage control than achievement.

And—let's be practical about this—if, after reading it, this book fails to help you gain perspective on the upheaval in your own life, then I suggest you don't fold down the page corners, and don't spill any gravy on the cover; instead, put a birthday card on it and wrap it as a gift for someone else.

Now, lastly, because I have been accused from time to time of twisted representation, and in fairness to the many wonderful people in this book who have knocked the rough edges off my life, I offer the following:

DISCLAIMER

"We, the family of Lynn Jaynes, want you to know that she stretches the truth."

"You can't say that! It's not true. I wrote exactly what happened."

"NO, you didn't!"

"Well, I wrote the *spirit* of the things that happened. If I tell people *exactly* what happened, my point won't be clear enough."

"And what's the point?"

"The point is, this is *my* view of things."

"Well *that* explains a lot, but just *for the record,* we want people to know you lie."

"I embellish. Perhaps I stretch things a tad. Maybe."

"You fabricate."

"I decorate. I trim and ornament and adorn."

"You *exaggerate.*"

"Okay. *That's* a word I can live with. So noted. Happy now? I'd say it all again in a *heart* squeeze. Now run along so I can tell these nice people things as I see them."

Levi Jaynes   Homer Jaynes

Will Jay

Rachel Jaynes

DIRK

Jenny De Ford   Edward

And there you have it. My husband, five children, son-in-law, grandchildren, mother, siblings, and anyone else even remotely related take absolutely no responsibility for anything in this book—which is typical. They don't take responsibility for the wet towels on the bathroom floor, the dirty dishes in the family room, the unmowed lawn, or the empty milk jug in the fridge either.

Pleased to meet you.

SEASON I

A Little Girl in
a Big Girl's World

Sunday School: How I Learned About Faith

Sister Norma probably thought no one in her Sunday School class of ten-year-olds was listening. Much of the time we weren't. However, I remember one day when something made me sit up and pay attention.

"O-L-I-V-E-R C-O-W-D-E-R-Y."

There it was, written in yellow chalk on the blackboard of the classroom in the old Hollister ward house. I just stared at it, trying to comprehend it. Sister Norma, at the front of our class of three or four kids, had written it plain as day. Slowly, understanding began to seep into my little head. Oliver Cowdery. A man. One man. Amazing.

For the first nine years of my life when people said, "Oliver Cowdery," I heard, "All-of-her-cowdery." I didn't have a clue what a cowdery was, but it sounded like something akin to a cavalry—maybe a regiment of two or three hundred men. And, yes, I did think it was a little odd that they referred to Joseph Smith and his men in the feminine vernacular, but, hey, I was a kid. In my world, adults seldom did things that made sense.

For several years I just thought that Joseph Smith translated the Book of Mormon with a regiment of some two hundred men, received the priesthood with two hundred men, and that he was baptized with a cowdery of two hundred men. Until that momentous day in Sunday School, when with a piece of chalk and a blackboard Sister Norma straightened it all out for me, that's what I thought.

The mountain-moving fiasco was her fault, too. She taught us one Sunday about Peter and Jesus walking on water. She talked about having the faith to walk on water. And she also talked about the scripture that said that with faith we could move mountains. It became obvious to my ten-year-old mind that I had enough faith to move mountains—I was just sure of it. I was always hearing how children have loads of faith, usually even more than adults. So if I was going to try mountain moving, I thought I'd better get started right away. I was growing older by the minute, and my faith was probably oozing out of my pores at that very moment.

I went out behind my house and looked for a good mountain to practice on. I could only see a little hill not far from our house. It would have to do. But before I moved this hill I decided I'd better figure out where to set it (naturally you wouldn't want a mountain hanging in the air while you decided something like that). I looked around for a likely spot. The hay field to the east wouldn't do. I was pretty sure my dad would be upset about that. If I put it north on the potato field, it might mash the tractors. I couldn't see beyond the hill to the west, and I didn't want to set it down without knowing what I was setting it on, so that didn't seem like a good option. After all, what if someone was out there hunting rabbits and I squished them? The south end of the farm wasn't a possibility either. It had the pumps and the pond and the potato cellar on it, and I didn't think I could squeeze a mountain in amongst it all.

No matter how long I puzzled over it I couldn't quite work out the details of mountain moving. As I lay in my bed one night thinking about it, I caught sight of the bottle collection on my bedroom shelf. If only the scriptures taught bottle-moving before mountain-moving, like a graduated course, I thought to myself. Then it occurred to me that nobody had said I couldn't try my faith out on a bottle first. When I got the hang of it, I could move on to mountains. Yes, of course—that was my answer.

I climbed out of bed and fetched one of my perfume bottles off the shelf. I placed it on the far end of my dresser. Then I prayed. I explained to my Heavenly Father, as only a ten-year-old could, what I was doing. I asked Him to move the bottle to the other end of the dresser for me, because of my faith. Then I got up, climbed into bed, and waited for morning (I thought maybe Heavenly Father might need all night to work on it). But when I awoke, much to my disappointment, my bottle was unmoved. I didn't understand why.

One night as I soaked in the bathtub, I was pondering Sister Norma's faith lesson and the bottle-moving business. All that water around me reminded me of how Peter had walked on water because he had lots of faith. Now, a bathtub isn't even close to being a canal, or a pond, or even a ditch, let alone a sea, but frankly, I was already in the bathtub, and I figured once again that maybe I'd better start small. So, kneeling in the tub, I said my prayer and explained to Heavenly Father what I was doing, and asked for His help. Then I balanced myself on the sides of the tub and I carefully placed my feet just *on* the water. Of course, as soon as I put any weight on them, they went right through the water. Try as I might—one foot at a time, or both feet together—I still kept sinking to the bottom of the tub. And I didn't understand why.

I began listening to Sister Norma's lessons more carefully, always searching for some tidbit—something I must have missed. I kept trying to figure out how faith worked *exactly.* So far I had only learned that Heavenly Father wasn't particularly interested in moving perfume bottles or in helping little girls walk on water in the bathtub. As the Sundays rolled by I gradually forgot about mountain-moving, water-walking and such, but not about faith.

Many of my prayers and pleadings have been answered over the years, some instantaneously—even miraculously. Some have not. For a long time it seemed almost like I had a cord with a short in it. I never knew for sure when my prayers would work and when they wouldn't. But I kept at it, always hoping I could someday figure out what kind of faith it took to move mountains.

Then one Sunday, a Gospel Doctrine teacher finally explained faith, and what it took to make it work, in a way that suddenly made sense to me. He quoted from *Lectures on Faith:*

"Let us here observe, that three things are necessary in order that any rational and intelligent being may exercise faith in God unto life and salvation.

"First, the idea that he actually exists.

"Secondly, a correct idea of his character, perfections, and attributes.

"Thirdly, an actual knowledge that the course of life which he is pursuing is according to his will. For without an acquaintance with these three important facts, the faith of every rational being must be imperfect and unproductive; but with this understanding it can become perfect and fruitful."

I was pretty sure I had rational intelligence—probably even had it in Sister Norma's class at that young age. I also had (1) an idea that God actually existed; and (2) a fairly correct idea of His character, perfections, and attributes. (I'm not saying these were perfect, only that I had a good start on them.) But it was number three that hung me up: "an actual *knowledge* that the course of life which *[I am]* pursuing *is according to his will*" (emphasis added).

That's why the bottle wouldn't move. That's why both feet kept sinking to the bottom of the tub. That's why my electrical prayer cord sometimes worked and sometimes didn't—I hadn't figured out *His will.* A very important ingredient. What is His will?

If God's work and glory is "to bring to pass the immortality and eternal life of man" (Moses 1:39), then prayers to move perfume bottles probably aren't going to figure into that equation anytime soon.

It takes me a long time to figure some things out, and I'm working on the mountain-moving equation even now. When Moroni wrote that the brother of Jared moved a mountain, (Ether 12:30) he could have mentioned *why* the mountain needed to be moved and *why* it was the will of God that he do so. Was it in the way? In the way of what? Was it covering up something that needed to be revealed? Did it need to cover up something bad or wicked? What aspect of "the immortality and eternal life of man" did that fulfill?

So I still have questions, but I feel like I'm on the right track. And one thing is sure. I won't be relying on Joseph Smith's cowdery of two hundred men to explain it to me.

Womenfolk:
My Mother's Friends

When we were growing up, every community had a women's club. There is nothing more universal than womenfolk gathering to chat. I'll bet Eve even held a club in the Garden of Eden with the birds and bees (and maybe even the snake). My mom belonged to a ladies' club when I was little. "Club" was all we called it. In our community, the ladies, their kids, and sometimes even their cats were welcomed once a month into a member's home that had been scrubbed clean—from the light fixtures and drapery rods to the base-boards and chair legs. It would have been unthinkable for it not to have been. After all, a woman's home was her pride and joy; if it hadn't smelled of lemon oil and Clorox, it would have been a violation of the unwritten code of the Club. There were those home-makers who couldn't begin to dust under piled collections of seven-year-old home-and-garden magazines. These ladies always elected to hold Club at the local community church hall instead.

I loved seeing the different homes when we went to Club. I was in awe of the huge butterflies made of wallpaper that some hung on their walls, and the glass bunches of grapes on their coffee tables. And coasters . . . we didn't have coasters at our house. Each month I couldn't wait for the chance to tell Mom I had to use the bathroom; I could then walk through other parts of the house—and maybe peek in the bedrooms. When I got to the bathroom I would feel very grown up as I used the carefully folded towels (which didn't even have toothpaste smeared across them like ours usually did), and broke in the brand-spanking-new bar of scented soap that was always resting on the sink for the guests. I may have been only four or five years old, but *I* was a guest.

The hostess would always lay out her very best china dishes, borrow folding chairs from the local church, and use freshly ironed table linens, upon which sat bowls of sugar wafers and plates of dainty pastries for the guests. These homes often smelled faintly like old coffee, which worried me just a tad. I would wonder how much trouble I was in with God just for smelling coffee.

I suppose I have Club to thank for the many little tea parties I held at home as a child. It's probably why my favorite toy growing up was the miniature china tea set my grandma gave me for Christmas.

Mother always made me wear petticoats and dresses when I went with her to Club. She would put my hair in a ponytail ribbon and plaster back the sides with Dippity-do. In my best dress I practiced crossing my legs like the other ladies, even though they were usually wearing one hundred percent double-knit polyester pantsuits, which in the '60s were popular even though they had the texture of steel wool. The neighbor lady who'd emigrated from England even wore gloves to match her polyester; it made her double-knit seem so much more elegant.

These gatherings were special and solemn occasions. They required nut cups with pansy stickers on them. They required using great-grandma's silver sugar cup and linen napkins. They required doilies. They also required bingo. After each roll call and poem-reading session, the guests were invited to play bingo while the hostess prepared coffee, punch, and pastries. This was my favorite part. This was why I endured the dresses and Dippity-Do. I would sit on the floor at mother's feet, looking shy, while bingo cards and pinto-bean markers were passed around. Two prettily wrapped packages in the middle of the coffee table were the prizes, one for the adult bingo winner and one for the children's winner. I loved bingo. It was like having a birthday.

I always tried to be so careful with my beans, but they were constantly rolling off the card. I knew where the "free" space was, but I didn't know my numbers and letters yet. The ladies thought it was cute and always offered to help me. Lisping Mrs. Roberts and wrinkly Mrs. Kunkel were the nicest. They helped me find B-11 and G-52 and coached me when to say "Bingo!" They told me how wonderful my freckles were and told my mother how well I behaved. I pretended not to hear and tried hard to concentrate on keeping my beans on the card.

Finally, refreshments would be served—beautiful desserts—and not on paper plates, either. The ladies used sculpted-glass plates with matching clear-glass cups. It was the height of culture in rural southern Idaho.

I surreptitiously watched the ladies at Club and eavesdropped on their conversations as they politely sipped coffee and dabbed at their lipstick with napkins. I was fascinated by the way Mrs. Boss tucked hankies into her watch for safekeeping, even after she had just dabbed her nose with them. Wasn't that germy or something?

I guess ladies chat at the office these days. Ladies' clubs seem to be a thing of the past. It's sad in a way. Last week I saw sculpted glass plates and matching cups in an estate auction. I kicked myself for not buying them. But I still have one teacup and matching saucer from my childhood tea set. It's cracked. It's not worth anything—except to me, to remind me of the days I was a little girl in a party dress.

It seems to me that many values were instilled upon me in my childhood through the conversations my parents had with other adults. Eavesdropping I think it's called. What a tragedy that neighborhood visiting has gone by the wayside. Where are kids supposed to eavesdrop if parents don't visit? How do parents instill values in their children if parents don't whisper them to someone else? Kids listen to whispers. I know eavesdropping is supposed to be a bad thing, but I'm thinking that it's also a really valuable tool. I certainly learned what farmer's wives valued when I eavesdropped at Club. I learned their attitudes, their political leanings, their backgrounds and their quirks. I learned that one didn't discuss family or business finances freely, or irrigation water issues—even then they steered clear of water issues.

Yes, I'm thinking I should remind myself to visit more and whisper to other adults more, and take my grandchildren with me so they can eavesdrop. Through that medium I could just teach them a thing or two, and their parents wouldn't even be able to chastise me for butting in. How perfect is that?

It wouldn't surprise me a bit if, as a little spirit in heaven just waiting to come to earth, I'd eavesdropped on Adam and Eve as they talked with God in the Garden of Eden. How else would I know God loved me?

How Old Are the Hills, Anyway?

Age is a funny thing—hard to determine sometimes. A few years ago I had only to look at frumpy middle-aged women to decide they were old. Now I *is* one! Middle aged, that is. I'm still in denial about the frumpiness. Maybe the age of things should be determined by the sum of their parts. If I take a fifteen-year-old car and add a twelve-year-old engine block to it, does that make the car twenty-seven? Or should the ages be averaged—thirteen and a half? Maybe age is utterly irrelevant. Irrelevant to everybody except middle-aged women and children, anyway. And as an eight-year-old, it was imperative to me that the world make sense.

In the foothills of the Sawtooth Mountains, a dowdy little homesteader's house has for years been decaying board by board, shingle by shingle. Two nearly fossilized bachelors, Wally and Alvin, used to live there. It never seemed fit to call them Alvin and Wally, only Wally and Alvin. When I was about eight years old, our family called on Wally and Alvin regularly. I think they were Dad's home-teaching assignment, but in any case, it was the neighborly thing to do.

I often debated with myself about what was the oldest: the house, the hills, Wally, Alvin, or their three-legged dog, Happy. The hills, the house, Happy, Wally, and Alvin all wheezed, groaned, and eroded a little more with every storm and rain shower. I tried picturing Happy as a pup, the frame house as newly built, the hills as newly squeezed steaming lumps of earth, and Wally and Alvin as being young—or at least not old, smelly, and decrepit. I wrestled with the evidence at each visit.

Shy Alvin always met us at the door. Silent and grave, he would lead us inside, past the rabbit and coyote skins hanging from rafters on the porch. We stepped around malnourished calves chewing frayed curtains—yes, inside—or eating through a box of Cheerios on the back porch. Then it was through mountains of old newspapers, gopher traps, and broken furniture into the kitchen. At least, it must have been a kitchen. I recognized a sink with a faucet (which I assumed meant running water) and a wood cookstove. In all the times I visited Wally and Alvin, I never dared look closely at the piles of dirty pots and pans for actual edible food. The smell of dog biscuits mixed with bacon fat never went away, and the thought of what I might find beyond the spider webs and mice rice was just too scary.

Wally would be waiting in a stiff leather chair in the living room with Happy. Happy was half blind, forever shedding, and ugly. The dog had only three legs. It did occur to me to wonder whether Wally and Alvin had eaten the other leg. Surely not. But maybe it was hanging on the porch with the coyote and rabbit skins.

Yellowed wallpaper and crumbling lath and plaster had fallen in piles around the living room. A dirty string attached to the pull-chain of a single bare lightbulb hung from the ceiling, often brushing my face as I stepped over Happy, sending shudders up my spine. I remember moving a stack of 1940 *National Geographic* magazines to sit on the very lip of a chair, careful not to lean back and touch too much.

"How the heck are ya?" Wally bellowed. (Though it wasn't quite "heck" when it came out time after time.) Clearly Wally and Alvin were not the typical home-teaching family. Wally was hard of hearing, and his bellowing made his pencil-thin legs shake. His sunken eyes and protruding bones reminded me of a skeleton. Dirt and grime made his denim jeans and flannel shirt (buttoned clear to the top) as stiff as a board. The clothes were not faded, though— they had probably never been washed. I suspected it was only the stiffness of his clothes that kept Wally himself standing upright. In third grade we had learned a song about Methuselah that went, "Them bones, them bones, them—dry bones . . ." Well, Methuselah had nothing on Wally.

Wally also had asthma. As he bellowed out conversations with my dad, he would occasionally lean over a glass dish and breathe deeply of a burning, acrid incense that opened up his lungs. I thought his lungs obviously worked just fine, and the incense didn't seem to have any effect on the rattling noise emanating from under the flannel shirt as Wally and Dad talked about cow markets and whether there was enough feed on the hills.

I peered up at the dim, smoky family pictures in oval frames on the walls. Mom had told me they were of Wally's wife and parents. Hmm . . . parents. So Wally must actually have been a baby once. That thought was a stumper.

"Alvin! Alvin! Darnit, Alvin, git these folks some candy," Wally bellowed. (The bellow, once again, included a different version of "darnit.") I was convinced Alvin couldn't see well because of the whitish glaze over most of his eyes and the red rim circling them. A schoolmate of mine used to invert his eyelids to make the girls "oooh" and "aaah." That's how Alvin looked all the time. He never spoke, never smiled, and he always obeyed Wally. Straight strands of gray hair stuck up around his shirt collar and out his ears. It looked itchy. Dad insisted Alvin was smart and could fix anything. But he didn't look smart to me.

As ordered, Alvin produced a box of chocolate-covered cherries and offered them to us kids, one by one. Remembering Mom's manners lessons, I reached for a chocolate. I knew I would never eat it, but planned to stow it in my pocket supposedly "for later." Then I saw a weevil worm crawling over the candies. Alvin averted his eyes. Stomach acids rose in my throat. In spite of the scolding I knew would be waiting at home, I politely whispered, "No, thank you," and concentrated on waiting for the visit to end.

We kids all held our breath as we passed the porch once more, waiting for the fresh air outside before we resumed inhaling. In the front garden, weeded-over flower beds choked the window frames where someone had once meticulously gathered rock borders and planted now-wild rosebushes. Nearly petrified cow pies (and fresh ones too) partially masked the little rock borders where they had been kicked aside. A few sporadic tulips and violets dared to live, but randomly, as if afraid to call attention to themselves. Remnants of a picket fence hung like broken teeth—victim of the cows, no doubt. No one now tended this little garden with love, yet the evidence of younger days was there—hints of hollyhock and mown grass clutched at it. Somewhere around back a generator hummed in the evenings, accompanying our departure as we all trooped to the car for the ride home. I would remain quiet, pondering the clues I'd gathered.

For the most part, I could arrange ages this way: Wally (because he was wheezing so hard to breathe) was obviously dying, so he must be the oldest. Alvin was next oldest—younger than Wally because he could still walk. Happy, the three-legged dog, didn't fit anywhere, but at least I knew he had one foot in the grave already. The house must be younger still, because the lone tulips and violets in the yard still *wanted* to live. That left only the hills.

To a ten-year-old mind, the age of the hills wasn't difficult. The hills were younger than the house, and Wally, and Alvin. They smelled new and fresh—like breath and life, not death. Green and growing sagebrush, rabbit brush, chokecherries, and serviceberries fought over them. Ants battled invaders on them. Water ran through them. Promising fish ponds rippled in them. Birds sang about them. The hills breathed and pulsed. Of course they were the youngest. I had it all figured out.

Then on a snowy, wintery day in 1972, on a snowbank among Wally and Alvin's hills, my time line melted. Our family invited Wally and Alvin, and we hauled up snowmobiles and saucer sleds on this visit so we could spend the day sliding down the mountainside— cold, wet, and screaming our guts out. Wally sat in a pickup at the bottom of the hill—he had the window rolled down and the heater going full-bore. We kids were dressed like abominable snowmen in layers of goose-down overalls, but were still numb from the cold. Alvin stood statuelike at the top of the hill in a simple denim jacket, hands in his pockets, never shivering, never smiling, never speaking, never looking anyone in the eye.

"Come on, Alvin, try the sled," we begged. I'm not sure why we pestered him; he didn't respond. He remained completely expression- less. We must have just assumed anyone would want to have as much fun as we were, screaming bloody murder as we plunged toward soft, wet pain at the bottom. Either that, or we just enjoyed goading him.

"Come on, Alvin, it's your turn!" Alvin only remained standing silently. Not really expecting him to change his mind, we quickly jumped on the sled again, rushed headlong to the bottom of the hill in a cloud of white spray, and overturned, catching faces full of ice. It was glorious. The hills echoed with shouts and the sputtering of snowmobiles.

The snowmobiles were pulling as many of us to the top as they could in one trip, but impatient to try another tumble, I climbed the hillside on foot instead, sinking to my knees with every step. I was breathless and sweating by the time I reached the top. The sledding path was packed now and very slick as I headed down the hill. I plowed through another fifteen feet of snow along the top, when suddenly, ricocheting through the hills, I heard Wally bellowing even more loudly than usual.

"Alvin! Alvin! WHAT ARE YOU DOING?"

I turned in time to see Alvin airborne on his way down the hill, not a sled in sight. In a cloud of white, our balding, red-eyed Alvin tumbled toward the bottom of the hill down our steep sledding trail. It was over in seconds. He landed in a silent, ungainly heap at the bottom. Snow absolutely covered him, all except—what was that—a smile? I froze, and it wasn't because of the cold. Wally didn't sound stunned, though. He only grew louder.

"Alvin, what do you think you're doing? Darnit, you're no kid, you know. Now you quit that! What's gotten into you? Get off that hill!" Wally bellowed for a good five minutes, without taking a breath, it seemed. Alvin just stood and dusted himself off, then shoved his hands back in his pockets and took Wally's battering silently—but took it with a smile, he did.

I had to make a new time line that day. Alvin must be younger than the house, younger than the three-legged dog, younger than Wally, and younger even than the hills, because, I reasoned, Alvin had apparently just that day started to live. So, once again, my world made sense.

There's not much I can do about being middle-aged now (sigh); however, on an eternal scale my spirit is still young. I won't wait until I'm as old as Alvin was to "start" living. And I don't think I'll let my spirit die when I'm young, like Wally seemed to. And when the snow starts flying I will definitely find me a good steep snowbank, bundle up my grandkids and race them to the bottom of the slope. For that matter, I may not wait for the grandkids. I might just go myself.

Driving Lessons:
Finding My Conscience

October is just the very best. The days aren't so bloomin' hot, the grass only has to be mowed once a week, and it's easier to club the grasshoppers among dying weeds than thriving ones. Autumn is the best in every way but one—every fall I must do penance.

It was innocent enough—an accident really. In October 1976, my sister Marcia and I were winding up a winning high school volleyball season. Life was good. However, there was an elderly widow woman in our neighborhood, Emma, who obviously didn't keep track of inconsequential things like teenagers' volleyball seasons. She thought only about things like dirty windows, spiderwebs in the corners, and Lawrence Welk. I know this because twice a month my mother volunteered my sister and me to help Emma out with odd household duties. I don't use the word "odd" lightly. The chores she put us to meant spending a half hour watering the African violets under a special lamp, vacuuming carpets which still had visible vacuum tracks from the previous vacuuming, and swatting at imaginary spiderwebs in the corners.

It might not have been so bad except that her house wasn't even mildly interesting—no knickknacks, no hobbies, no family paraphernalia. And a trip to her house always included sitting down with her to watch Lawrence Welk—teenager torture. I always felt like I was wasting my valuable time and considerable talents whenever I was "helping" Emma. As far as I could see, she didn't need help anyway—at least, not the help of a teenager.

Marcia and I usually took turns going to her house, but on one particular October afternoon Marcia pulled rank and insisted it was

my turn to do the Emma-duty, even though I clearly remembered
doing it the last time. That meant leaving volleyball practice early to
drive to Emma's, because Emma had to get to bed by 8:30 P.M. I was
mad. (I know redheads don't *usually* get mad—but I made an excep-
tion.) It *wasn't* my turn. It *wasn't* fair. It wasn't even *necessary.*

I think that's why I took the turn too fast. Turning from the pave-
ment onto the loose gravel of a country road could be tricky anyway,
but did you know that in a large, buslike, old, green Suburban you
can actually get liftoff? And where that stop sign suddenly came from
I have noooo idea . . . but I killed it. Killed it dead. Decapitated it. A
clean break. (It also left a nice, clean dent in the hood of the family
car, but frankly that didn't worry me since—due to my four older
brothers and sisters—the car had several dents already and no one was
going to notice one more.)

But surely somebody would notice the stop sign. Surely. However,
I wouldn't have to own up to it. I wasn't sure how serious an infrac-
tion murdering a stop sign was, but it could only be bad news. Telling
my parents might necessitate telling the highway department or the
sheriff's office, and my car-insurance rates might go up. Then I'd have
to constantly hear about that from my parents—and who had time
for that? I had a volleyball season to think about. Yes siree bob, this
could just be my little secret.

I just had no idea at the time how those little secrets can strangle
a mind. At least twice a day I had to pass that spot where the stop
sign wasn't—sometimes more. And *each and every time,* I wondered if
someone would miss the stop because the sign wasn't there, and crash,
and get hurt, and need to be extricated from the vehicle with the Jaws
of Life, and get taken to the hospital, and need blood transfusions, X-
rays, and MRIs, and maybe a transplant, and then get life-flighted to
Salt Lake and lie in a coma with a broken neck and eleventy-seven
broken ribs, tragically vegetative in an iron lung (whatever that was),
and have to be fed through stomach tubes, and wither away, and
months later finally expire, leaving behind a brokenhearted husband
who visited her daily and wept poignantly at her bedside while
remembering their tender times together—including their first
romantic kiss and courtship, and the birth of their two young children who would now be left for someone else to raise, and who

would never even remotely remember their mother, and who would have no one to help them learn to tie their shoes or help them blow out birthday candles or to read nursery rhymes and sing lullabies to them at night. And then there was the funeral . . . and I would be responsible for all of it.

Every time I passed the spot where the stop sign wasn't, I added a new line to the story. I read the papers for car-crash headlines. I listened to AM radio news. I felt sick from the top of my stomach to the bottom of my volleyball blisters.

It took two weeks, four days, and seventeen hours for someone to finally notice there wasn't a stop sign at the intersection and to plant a new one. Negligent if you ask me. Taxpayers pay a lot of good money for the superintendent of stop signs to take that criminally long to notice. Shameful. But not as shameful as my behavior.

And that is why every October has a blotch on her beautifully cool, cider-smelling, leaf-turning days. There is always at least one day each fall that I do penance for not telling the truth about the assassinated stop sign.

SEASON II

Raising My Own Family

Tangles of Nightshade, Morning Glory, and Kids

"I'll give you six bucks for those two goslings," my son Homer told the clerk. I beamed. This kid had picked up something from me, after all. We had gone to the feed-and-seed store to buy onion sets, seed potatoes, and tomato plants for that year's garden, and the penned-up goslings in the back of the store did look tempting. The store clerk was unmoved.

"No, they're six bucks apiece, like the sign says."

Homer tried again. "Yeah, but you'll never get rid of all twenty. I'll take two of them off your hands for six bucks." How could this clerk not be swayed by such a handsome, persistent seventeen-year-old boy?

"I'm sorry," was all the clerk said.

I was partly relieved, but of course Homer was disappointed. As we gathered up our brown seed bags for the garden and headed for the car, I realized I'd never told Homer about how all this—these goslings and all this garden seed—started with his Aunt Jane, and a milk cow we shared, named Elsie.

Jane and I are just two garden-variety sisters who were raised on an Idaho farm. We both married and later ended up living side by side. Jane and Calvin bought the milk cow first—Elsie. They shared her with us. Jane milked in the mornings and I milked in the evening. Elsie gave us enough milk for both families and raised a couple calves besides. When Jane and Calvin could afford the calves, they bought them at the auction and grafted them onto Elsie. When they couldn't afford to buy calves, then Fred and I did.

One day Jane and Calvin needed cash for something or other, and so Fred and I bought Elsie for five hundred dollars. Elsie never knew it, of course. She grazed in the same pasture, was milked on the same schedule, occasionally kicked over the same old tin milk bucket, and swished her tail at the same old barn flies. Some months later Fred and I were pinched for cash. So Jane and Calvin bought Elsie back—five hundred dollars. Again, Elsie never changed pastures and her routine was never interrupted.

I don't know how many times Jane and I changed ownership of Elsie, but it was enough times that one day we laughed because we couldn't remember who owned her. It didn't matter; by that time we shared pretty much everything—pig-raising projects, chicken raising, rabbit raising, garden raising, and even children raising. More than once her kids came in to ask what I was fixing for supper. And if I said, "Beef liver," they inevitably trotted out the door and across the field to Jane's house to ask her what she was fixing for supper. Pretty soon I'd hear a giggling little girl's voice on the phone asking, "Can Rachel eat dinner at our house?"

We had enough kids that keeping them all busy and productive required lots of projects and chores. Hence, we had lots of animals. When no chores were handy, we'd have to create a few.

The garden was Jane's idea. I personally thought we should wait until we were a lot more desperate before turning to gardening. Even though the prophets have admonished us to garden, I don't recall them ever saying we had to like it. Nonetheless, gardening would teach the kids responsibility, so I had to acquiesce. One sunny morning in May, Jane and I lined up our families to outline their gardening duties. Jane began. Heading her lineup was her husband Calvin, followed by their kids—Trevor, Trent, Cali, Abe, Ty, and Ande. She approached them with her uniquely tolerant and patient manner: "Okay, this will be so much fun! We'll sing songs while we hoe, play name-that-bird while we plant the seeds, and memorize scriptures while we weed the rows. Everybody will have a job and will be expected to do his job every day. Calvin, you're excused to the barn until you can smile and be happy." She didn't have to tell her husband twice—he was gone in a flash.

My family was next and I approached them with a drill sergeant's finesse: "Fred (my husband), Jenny, Homer, Will, Levi, Rachel—QUIT HIDING AND GET OUT HERE RIGHT NOW!" They came sulkily, but they came. I continued, "Alright, here's the deal. It costs a ton to feed us all year, and this garden will help our grocery budget. If you expect to eat, then you'd better help with the garden. And Fred, you may *not* be excused to go to the barn with Calvin. If I have to suffer, then you do too."

Over the ensuing summer (and for many summers afterward), our families padded barefoot up and down the garden rows. I confess that Calvin and Jane's family did most of the work, but I never completely gave up either, and that was my small victory.

As for Jane's family, Calvin took over the chore of watering because no one else could do it quite to his satisfaction. Cali liked picking caterpillars from the leaves; one summer she went through the corn patch peeling husks on the tender, immature stalks looking for caterpillars until every single ear of corn was exposed. But she had a great caterpillar collection. Trevor and Trent hid in the corn at night so they could spook the bejeebies out of everybody. Abe was pretty fair at weeding—if the person ahead of him had a book strapped to his hind-end—and Ty was the best potato-bug squisher I ever saw. Together they tramped out many corn-stalk forts after harvest. Ande was too young to be much help, but she was responsible for bringing Kool-Aid, which she did admirably.

As for my family, Fred took turns discing and harrowing on the little garden tractor—round, and round, and round, and round again. If it ever looked like we needed some *real* work done, he would insist there was more tractor work to do. Jenny had the nerve to enjoy weeding in the early morning and so always got her work done quickly. For his part, Homer tried to keep the crows away with his BB gun and also set gopher traps. Will and Levi mostly just had clod fights, but liked weeding the carrots and peas best because they could eat them as they went. Rachel helped with the singing. Her operatic rendition of "I Am a Child of God" was especially entertaining.

The garden itself was marginally successful—better some years than others. One year all the beans sprouted on time, but when they blossomed the leaves immediately curled and looked sickly—a withered yellow, not the healthy green they should have been. Even Jane's faith seemed to falter. She wondered why, if we were trying to raise responsible children and be more self-sufficient, the Lord wasn't blessing this effort. *You should have seen it if I hadn't blessed it,* was immediately impressed upon her mind. And then, even when it looked so hopeless, the beans that year produced on into a late Indian summer, so abundantly that we had to call in neighbors to cart them away.

Our families eventually moved apart. And some of our kids have now grown and left home. But despite the miles between us, we know it's important to stay connected. We still try to achieve separately the family values we tried to accomplish together, and that's why Homer was buying garden seeds with me again. As usual, I'm late planting, and do it more out of guilt than a love for growing things. That could be why my garden is still a tangle of nightshade and morning glory. Jane's, however, is still in nice, neat, weedless rows, and she's still singing. Our philosophies don't vary, though; we both know gardens (like families) take lots of work.

Like our country gardens, our families sometimes grew in straight rows and sometimes in clumps. They produced beautiful flowers and delicious produce, but they were also choked with weeds at times. But one thing is sure: At any given time our families were and are growing, changing, and, if well tended, producing. No matter if the goose eats the pea blossoms or the mules trample it underfoot, the garden is still ours, and we will keep nourishing and weeding it. Because that's what families do.

The Money Bone: Developing My Own Investment Portfolio

"Invest!" Grandpa told me. "Instead of working for money, make money work for you." He knew all too well what money (and the lack thereof) could do to a body. He'd had a young family when the Great Depression hit. However, he was fortunate; he worked in construction, building roads and airports and such for the government, so during the Depression he actually made money. He believed in money; believed in making it—he was born with what we came to call a "money bone."

Apparently the money bone was not hereditary. That's not to say I haven't had experience with money and investments. Quite the contrary.

When our five children were small and wanted money for candy, we tried the usual household-chores-for-allowance thing. It is a good concept in theory, but our execution was flawed. Supervising the money-chores only doubled my own daily workload and (of course) cost me money at the same time. Actually, it cost me double. The children were so small they just played with the coins they earned, so in order to teach tithing we had to do things like suck the coins from the heating vents so they'd have something to give the bishop. They never had enough collected coins to buy anything for themselves. I guess they were really too young to appreciate payment in forms other than a Popsicle, anyway. Only nickels and dimes were involved, but this minor financial loss was only the first of many.

As most people know, when kids grow, so do their wants and needs. That's when we discovered dividends. Somehow, as the kids grew, the family budget seemed to shrink proportionately. We began to look for income alternatives outside the family. One of our first plans consisted in pulling cockleburs from a bean field. We were to be paid by the acre. I knew the going would be slow with little children, but I thought with glee of how tired they'd be by noon. It didn't occur to me, at the time, that I'd be tired as well. We arose every morning at 6:30 A.M. and fought stickers, thistles, gnats, and mud-packed feet until it got too hot. I lost money buying the kids soda and bubble gum, but as a family we also got to sing some really dumb songs and recall every knock-knock joke we'd ever heard. We chased rabbits and played a few games of hide-and-seek among the vines. I'd never really lived until I'd lain flat on my back in a corrugate with a ladybug on my upper lip, afraid to move for fear of being discovered by a six-year-old. I've owned mutual funds that didn't pay that well.

I wish my grandpa could have seen us when we started the next summer's "get-rich-worming" project. We bought worming prods and coolers, and we set aside gas money for trips to town. We ended up losing money right and left, but we *felt* rich. It was a project five-year-old Levi could fully appreciate. One evening he stretched a night crawler between his two hands and said, "Look, Mom, a worm!" He kept stretching his hands farther and farther apart; the worm grew thinner and thinner, and Levi's eyes grew more astonished. Then . . . POP! "Look, Mom, *two* worms!" Later a sparrow landed on the nearby grass, hungrily watching us harvest worms. I watched Levi choose a long, juicy worm out of the bucket and toss it over to the sparrow. On the average, I only lost about five dollars per week, and I gained a little boy who learned persistence and sweet generosity.

Our next unprofitable venture was raising baby calves on a nurse cow. I don't know how much we earned, but eleven-year-old Homer (the wannabe teenager) learned to milk, growing proud of the strength in his grip and the bulging veins in his arms. Twelve-year-old Jenny (the I-hate-cows-do-I-have-to-smell-them-too? daughter) learned that if she folded enough laundry she could avoid the milking barn altogether. Little four-year-old Rachel learned that she could have my undivided attention for forty whole minutes if she parked herself on a hay bale beside the cow when it was my turn to milk. She would tell me all about her dolls and kittens, and how unfair it was to have to share her bedroom with an older sister. As she sat telling me her woes, my heart considered the venture profitable, even if my pocketbook didn't.

Another adventure (by then we had quit calling them "ventures") was mowing lawns. We spent four hundred dollars for a lawn mower, fully aware that if the boys ran over a dog dish just once, the mower would be destroyed. But when Homer (the am-I-a-teenager-yet? son) showed Will (the my-arm-hurts-from-getting-socked-by-Homer son) how to change the lawn-mower oil, and as they cooperated in raking grass clippings together, I felt this, too, was profitable. Of course, when they were finished they had to argue about whose hatband had soaked up the most sweat, but at least they were arguing about who *did* the most work and not who *didn't*.

We invested in "bonds" next. For three years running we delivered phone books with the goal of using the funds for a swimming pass at the local pool. One year we delivered over sixteen hundred books. We concluded that project with five worn-out pairs of sneakers, an empty bottle of aspirin, and five children who collapsed into deep sleep at 6:00 P.M. and would not be roused the next morning even by the thought of cartoons and cold cereal with marshmallows. Although we earned enough to buy the swim pass, Grandpa would have pointed out that the dent in the bumper from backing into a mailbox was not conducive to profit margins. But you can't place a value on singing along with your children to the car radio while using your thumbs for microphones. And how do you put a price on learning a strong work ethic? We definitely acquired bonds, if not in the financial sense.

Helping the kids "earn" money was exhausting. I might have given up if I hadn't taken courage from a statement by Sister Flora A. Benson, who said, "We have often told our children, 'We have little money to leave you, but of far greater value, we hope to leave you . . . a rich heritage, a good name and clean bodies, and a love and respect for honest work.'"

With that in mind, we even tried the "stock" market, buying cute little baby chickens. What amazed me was how much feed a cute little-bitty chick, multiplied by one hundred and twenty-five, could eat. It stretched our family budget to the edge. But Homer nursed the tiny birds whenever they fell into the water, and carried a broken-legged chick from water to feed three times a day. This was the son who had struggled to control his temper, and learning compassion while caring for the chicks was a balm to his young spirit. I wouldn't trade the dividends we earned in that stock market for any number of pork barrels.

I will never be featured in the *Wall Street Journal.* My actual investment portfolio is still pathetically anemic. Even with all this experience behind me, I'm not competent at raising calves, raising chickens, or picking worms. But I have been earning interest. I wish my grandpa could see my little family now. These five lawn-mowing, phone-book-running, worm-picking great-grandkids of his are blooming just fine, despite the prosperity blight.

Don't Cry When I'm Gone, Mom

"Oh, I'd love to help clean out the shed, dear, but I'm quilting today," I told my husband. I thought it sounded rather noble, even matronly.

Actually, it was just an excuse to watch my children play. Stitch after stitch, their childhood unfolded before me. I chuckled at their costumed performances of "Finely Gowned Ladies at a PTA Meeting," or "Let's Pretend We're Barbies Shopping at D.I." I participated in their tea parties and played customer in their cafés. "No, you can't order that today," they'd say.

"Why not?" I'd ask.

"Because I can't spell it."

Heavy perfume and crooked lipstick always made me smile.

They settled the Wild West and cultivated carpet pile into fields of grain. They slam-dunked rolled up socks and spiked balloon volleyballs. They built forts with couch cushions and blankets. Quilting became much more than needlework. It was a chance to smell my roses.

My roses are all in school now. As the youngest prepared for her first-grade adventure, she said, "Now, don't cry when I'm gone, Mom."

I really wanted to be a big girl about it. I wanted to be as brave as my daughter. Hadn't I spent years preparing for this day? I consoled myself that I had plans for all kinds of projects—I'd only been waiting for a free moment: furniture to refinish, closets to clean, walls to paint, letters to write. Yet, somehow this paled in comparison to watching them swing from ropes in the barn, float boats in the ditch, run screaming through the sprinkler, and ride their bikes over dirt mounds.

I wondered what the next year would bring. They would learn more reading, English, math, and new catchphrases to call each other when they thought I wasn't listening. They would complain about their lunches and trade their fruit bars for cookies. Levi would be in second grade and would think he was being cheated because he didn't have a new watch for school. He religiously cut out watches from the Sunday newspaper ads for me. Never mind that he couldn't tell time yet. And I knew full well that in a few weeks Rachel would come home one day from kindergarten, never again to skip the number seventeen when she counted.

I wondered who would break up my day by asking me to make them chocolate milk. Whose "rrrruudddnnn, rrruuddddnnn" would I hear—or would I miss the dump trucks carting pinecones and driveway rocks through the house? Who would mother the dolls now left in their corners? Who would ask me to find something to put in her purse? Who would ask me if it's time to eat lunch at ten o'clock in the morning?

There was a flurry of activity that school morning before every child, including the youngest, boarded the school bus. We had gathered backpacks, packed lunches, and dug in closets for lost shoes and hair ribbons before they happily skipped off toward the school bus stop. I watched them jockey for a place in line to wait for the bus, laughing and talking. They finally boarded the bus and those folding yellow doors swallowed them up. I watched the bus for several more minutes as it lumbered down the road. Finding the house suddenly quiet, I sat down to quilt for a few minutes. As I sewed, one tear swelled after another. I guessed I wasn't going to be a big girl about this after all. Someday I would get around to those projects, but first I would quilt—and water my roses.

Wars of Independence

Just as there are Founding Fathers of this country, I am the Founding Mother and Fred is the Founding Father of this family. The Jaynes Family Constitution, as we see it, begins something like this:

We hold these truths to be self-evident, that all men are created equal, that they are endowed by their Creator with certain sacred and unalienable rights, that among these are Life, Liberty, and the Pursuit of Happiness. In pursuit of this happiness, you have the right to become an Eagle Scout, you have the right to hug your mom good night without embarrassment, and you have the right to give your mother a nicer gift on Mother's Day than you do your girlfriend on Valentine's Day. In exchange for these rights, your governing parents reserve the right to hold the disciplinary line even when you whine; they have the right to bench you at a basketball game for poor grades even when you are a starting player; and lastly, they reserve the right to cry unashamedly when you are sick or hurting, at your first haircut, your first piano recital, your first prom, your graduation, your wedding, or even at a pancake supper for no apparent reason at all. In summary, you have the right to love and be unconditionally loved in return. Until you're twenty-one and living on your own, you have no other rights whatsoever.
Signed,

The President and Her First Man

One day Homer said, "Mom, I'm almost fourteen." He paused before adding, "That means, according to the family rules, that I can hold hands with a girl."

Of course we had made those rules when the kids were maybe ten or twelve years old—long before that day became an actual possibility. We were young parents then. We didn't know any better. We'd had a moron moment.

When my heart stopped tap dancing, I called his bluff. "So, do you have in mind anyone's hand in particular, or are you just going to let all the girls take turns?"

"M-O-O-OM!" He rolled his eyes.

"Well, I just want to know if all the junior high girls are counting down the days until your fourteenth birthday too."

I think that's when it hit him—he didn't have a girlfriend. He didn't even have any prospects; he hadn't really looked for one. So this long-awaited, much-anticipated, prayed-for, begged-and-pleaded-for day was probably going to go by pretty much like any other. When it really came down to it, it didn't matter whether he actually held a girl's hand or not. It wasn't even the issue. What was important was that he had officially declared his independence. Declaring independence is not a new story. Our national Declaration of Independence may have been signed over 200 years ago, but the Jaynes Congress is still debating over the Jaynes Constitution. About this same time, Homer announced, "Mom, Dad. I am ready to move out for the summer and get a job riding cowboy on a ranch. *I'm thirteen years old.*"

Forthwith, his father and I reviewed with him some amendments to our Constitution or, as it will now be known, the "Jaynes Bill of Rights As It Applies to Thirteen-Year-Olds and Especially Homer."

Amendment I

"Freedom of religion" means scripture study begins at 6:00 A.M. sharp—and don't be late. "Freedom of speech" means you have the right to your own opinion as long as you mind your parents anyway, and "freedom of the press" means that before you move out of this house you *will* know how to press your own Sunday shirt.

Amendment II

"Freedom to keep and bear arms" means that arms *will* remain bare—no tattoos allowed.

Amendment III

No soldiers will be quartered in your room—but no rodents, reptiles, or insects, either.

Amendment IV

Protection against "unreasonable search and seizure" means you must empty your own pockets before they go through the washing machine, because it is unreasonable to expect this of your mother. Anything your mother does find in your pockets can and will be confiscated and/or held against you in a court of family law.

Amendment V

Protection from "double jeopardy" means that TV time is limited to one game show per week.

Amendment VI

The "right to a speedy trial" means that your trials include (but are not limited to) taking care of the calves on the nurse cow, straightening the porch, and irrigating the pasture. Should the inclination ever arise, you may even do it *speedily*.

Amendment VII

You may not sue family members, even over tapes that the boom box ate. "Suits in common law" refers to boys wearing suits, or at least white shirts and neckties, to church. It's the law.

Amendment VIII

No cruel and unusual punishment will be inflicted. Cleaning your own room, doing dishes, and emptying mousetraps are exceptions.

Amendment IX

These amendments are subject to review and change as soon as you become the parent.

Amendment X

The powers not herein delegated to children shall be discussed in family council with parents retaining the majority rule.

Amendment XI

This is the amendment that will remain flexible so that parents may make up new laws at any time, anyplace, and anywhere such occasions arise. Parents may repeal any moronic law they made when they were not thinking clearly. Today, this means simply no moving out at thirteen years of age to become a ranch hand.

The Songs They Make

One day recently, I was driving Rachel to town to buy school shoes. Almost a teenager, she wanted the newest thick-soled three-inch-high shoes, but I was pulling for the brown, sensible clodhoppers. I thought I was winning the argument when, suddenly changing the subject, she said, "Hey, Mom, want me to teach you a song?" Without waiting for an answer, she belted out, "Oooo-eeee-oooo-ah-ah-ting-tang-walla-walla-bing-bang . . ." and she was off. She didn't know this song had been around longer than I had; I learned it as a Beehive at girls' camp, and then again when I pretended not to know it as her older sister discovered it and wanted to teach it to me. Just as these thoughts began the familiar strains of a headache, a line from a poem by Nancy Baird came to mind: "To watch the child . . . Oh let it never end—listen to the song she makes!" So I listened to Rachel sing, feeling very tired and old. How many times in one lifetime must we experience things like that obnoxious song? I wondered. As I did so, I realized that each of my children seems to have at least one song of their own they want to teach me.

For example, on another day, when he was about four years old, Homer climbed on the piano bench and began banging away. I was peeling peaches in the kitchen until he yelled from the other room, "Hey, Mom, wanna hear my song about backhoes?" Curious, I dropped the peach peels in the sink and went into the family room to give him my undivided attention.

"I love backhoes. They're big. They're yellow. They have a bucket, we dig with them . . ." On and on he sang. He apparently couldn't carry a tune in a bucket, but he obviously didn't see that as a problem.

Usually the songs my children offer are not songs with instruments and voice. One January we were experiencing one of those weather inversions the weathermen like to tell us about but that nobody really understands. All we knew was that there was a lot of fog that froze in really cool sprinkles over the trees. I tried a simple explanation for three-year-old Homer's sake—that fog was nothing more than a cloud on the ground. Homer said, "A cloud on the ground? Isn't Jesus paying attention?" Maybe he had a point.

Later, Homer pretended to hunt deer with a homemade bow and arrow, and one day when I asked whether he'd gotten anything he said, "No, I decided to let them live." I smiled at the notion that he would have had a choice (if he'd actually seen any deer first off, and then given his vicious baling-twine bow, and the "speed" at which it could propel an arrow). Another time, when he was twelve years old, he decided to drive the pickup onto a pond of ice to see if it would break through.

On the whole, Homer's songs nearly wore me out.

Will's childhood world followed its own tune. He'd play for hours in the yard with toy tractors, humming away with his engine sounds. When it was cold outside, he'd come in and farm the shag carpet into fields until every carpet thread was evenly laid into rows. Will was also usually a little difficult to keep track of, and he often wandered off. To add to that, his imagination seeped out everywhere, like a pocket pen that always dribbles.

Will's songs were often in his head. When he slam-dunked a pair of rolled-up socks into a four-foot-high net, he heard the cheering crowds roar their applause. When he caught the balloon football in the front room and leaped over the couch for the touchdown, I chewed him out for jumping on furniture, but the fans in his imagination thundered at his end-zone dance.

Levi had a talent when it came to words. One day I was driving around a residential section of town with him when he saw a sign on the lawn of a very nice home that said, "For Sale. By Owner." He casually (and facetiously) asked, "I wonder why anyone would want to buy an owner?" When he was four years old he came running into the house to tell me about his fastest ride ever on a horse. All out of breath, he exclaimed, "I ran *so* fast, I was running forward and fifthward!"

Levi had a two-line ballad for nearly everything. One year we held family home evening on Mother's Day, and my husband Fred thought it would be great if the kids would all tell me a reason why they loved me. It was very nearly the longest, most difficult assignment of their young lives; they had a dickens of a time coming up with anything at all. They stammered and stuttered and thunk and thunk. Finally, Fred prompted them, and they came up with things like, "She cooks for me. She washes the clothes," etc. Then it was three-year-old Levi's turn. This was easy for him. "I don't love Mom. I love applesauce." It is, after all, tough to compete with applesauce.

Over the years Jenny's songs have taken more the tone of self-appointed instruction—"lecturing," if I weren't trying to be kind. And she was generous with her verses full of authority. It was five-year-old Jenny who patiently explained to her younger brothers that PINEapple comes from porcuPINES, and we have to pick up thumbTACKS off the floor because they can give us heart atTACKS. When she was six, she was assigned a talk for Sunday School. She meticulously colored a picture of a frog, held it up, and practiced over and over, "Jesus made the frogs. Jesus made the frogs." When Sunday came she stood at the pulpit, held up her picture, studied it a minute, then proudly announced, *"I* made the frog." Who could argue? It was certainly her handwriting and coloring.

That day in the car, Rachel reminded me it was her turn to sing. A few years ago, when she was five, she couldn't pass her kindergarten math assignments because she kept leaving out the number seventeen. "Who needs seventeen, anyway?" she'd say. Last month she turned twelve years old. She can't put the laundry piles in the bedrooms without pretending she's a poor, overworked waif who must fight valiantly for child-labor laws. Thanks to the PBS channel, she sings about her woes opera style, which doesn't include nearly as much style as tinny volume. And she's only twelve. I feel tired. She's my last child. It was wonderful, but hard, learning the songs of the other four. On the other hand, what great memories we share. I know if I don't hear Rachel's song I will have missed a big part of a mom's life.

That moment, in the car with her, I tried to forget my headache. I took a long breath and let it out slowly. "Okay, Rachel, how does it go? Teach me your song."

To watch the child . . . Oh let it never end—listen to the song she makes!

Confession

One day I went out to the barn to milk the cow; I found green spray paint everywhere. It was all over the fences, corrals, shop, barn, gates—anything that was eye level for a ten-year-old. There was something familiar about the handwriting, too.

When I went into the house, I said, "Will, I see a lot of green paint around the farm. Would you know anything about that?"

He thought about it, then replied, "How much trouble would I be in if I do?"

I chuckled to myself. "Oh," I said, "a lot less if you told me *right now* than if I found out on my own." Then he confessed.

One day Levi (who was about thirteen at the time) came into the house and sat beside me at the computer desk. He started this way: "Mom, let's suppose you had a child who had done something wrong, say about two-hundred-and-fifty-dollars'-worth wrong. How would that child tell you about that?"

"Well," I said, trying to keep a straight face, "I would probably tell Mom *real quick* and get it over with."

He hemmed and hawed a bit, but finally spit it out, "Well, I had the BB gun and was shooting at a bucket that was in the back of the pickup. One of the BBs ricocheted and broke the pickup window." Sure enough, when I went to assess the damage, the back window was in a billion pieces. Still, because he had come and confessed straightaway, I was able to keep my perspective.

Now, just occasionally, I do things wrong too—like about every time I clean the kids' bedrooms.

"Mom, I wish you'd quit cleaning my room!" Homer stormed.

"Why?" I tried to look innocent.

"Because now I can't find my deck of cards, or poker chips, or firecrackers."

"Hmm . . ." I was admitting nothing. At least not right away. "What did you do with them?"

"I don't know, but I know they were in that room somewhere before you cleaned it."

"Well, honey, if you'd clean your own room occasionally, I wouldn't have to." That wasn't a lie.

"That's not fair," he complained.

"It is in *my* house," I rejoined.

"Well, next time warn me before you clean."

"I don't think so."

And he stomped off mad and bought more cards and more firecrackers. But right away I noticed just how dirty his room was again. I was just going to have to clean it again. Those cards and firecrackers that I don't like one bit just seemed to clutter it up.

It's been awhile since the first time I cleaned his room, but, bless his heart, Will hasn't caught on yet. "Mom, I can't find that list of girls' phone numbers and addresses I had, or my new CD."

"Hmm . . ." I admitted nothing. "That CD I don't like?"

"Do you know where they went?"

"Well, I had to clean your room. Now let me think . . . how much trouble would I be in if I do?"

And he stomped off mad. I can't imagine why.

Then it's Levi's turn. "Mom, who took my *Calvin and Hobbes* books?"

"Hmm . . ."

"Well, who cleaned my room?"

"I did."

"Where did you put them then?"

"Gosh, I don't remember. But, if someone had given, say, about thirty dollars' worth of books to Deseret Industries, how would that person tell you about that?"

Used to this game, he gives in rather easily. "Now what am I going to read?"

"Well, I just happen to have a great novel that I think you'd really enjoy. Here—"

"It's five hundred pages!"
Yeah, I know. It should keep him busy all summer.

Hide-and-Don't-Seek

One day Lila (my sister) was hiding in the bushes next to her house to get a few minutes' peace from her family, and having fallen asleep, was presumed lost until eventually found by a search party of frantic neighbors. How embarrassing for her! Thank heaven, no one has ever found my hiding places. I'm assuming all women have them, of course. My sister Jane uses the closet, Lila has the bushes, and my little secret is the car—although it's a little nippy in cold weather. So, I can assume we're normal, right? Everybody has one? There's so little privacy for women, I can't imagine not having a hiding place.

I've tried the bathroom. It doesn't work. The quickest way to call a "family meeting" is for me to try to use the bathroom. As soon as my backside hits the cold porcelain, the commotion at the door becomes as loud and clamorous as the floor of the stock exchange. Someone urgently needs a shirt ironed, or a hem pinned, or to know if this shirt matches those pants. You'd think they could wait just a darn minute, or even ten. But they wait for nothing. The potatoes on the stove may boil over, and (incredibly) my children have time to run bang on the bathroom door to alert me before they think of taking a moment to turn the burner off! It's easy to see why movie directors often use the bathroom for climactic, chaotic scenes—more murders, more surprises, more crises happen there than any other room of the house. And I know why. It's a no-brainer! Open bathroom scene—insert crisis.

Don't try to find privacy in the bedroom, either. It's uncanny the way the whole family can hear my knees hit the floor for prayer. They wait until I start praying, and that's the exact moment I hear,

"MOOOOMM!" The Lord must be very weary of hearing me say, "Hang on a minute, will ya? That sounds like Levi, and I know it's rude of him to interrupt, but we're working on that. Please bless him anyway."

Somehow, only when it's 10:00 P.M. do the kids finally decide to dump all the rotten stuff that happened over the past twenty-four hours on me. And, oh yes, could I fix it all before 10:30? They bring cookies and popcorn and homework onto the bed, expect me to remember what a conjugate verb is, and want to know if I'd mind getting up to fix a pan of brownies while I think about it. And if I'm in bed, I mean really *in* bed—feeling groggy, pajamas, everything (not just faking it under the covers)—that's the time they decide they want a haircut.

So, as far as hideouts and privacy go, I can vouch that bedrooms and bathrooms are definitely out. The closets in my house can't even hold the Christmas decorations and camping gear, let alone me. I didn't fit in the doghouse. The storage room is just too creepy in the dark. (Of course, a good hideout has to be dark, so I can cry long and loud.) That leaves very few options.

That's why I eventually resorted to the car, at least in the summer months. It's dark, safe, soundproof, and if I scrunch down so no one can see me, it's private. Not only did I have some really decent cries in there, but with the aid of a flashlight, I even read Michener's *Hawaii* in the Suburban. I read *War and Peace* in the blue four-door. And I read Twain's *Short Stories* in the van. Getting *to* the car, however, is a little tricky, because one must avoid the dogs—the best hiding spot in the world is doomed if the dogs follow, sniffing and whining. However, the car is certainly better than hiding in trees. If I hide in the trees, the dogs lift their leg on nearly every one, and then I have to keep track so I'll know which trees not to lean against. Before you leave the house, and regardless of where you hide, it's very important to find out exactly where the dogs are, and wait for them to lie down peacefully before sneaking out.

Following are general tips for hiding spots which all women might find useful:

Tip #1: If you leave the back door open just a crack, no one actually hears you leave, and no one suspects you're going anywhere, thus no one panics or follows.

Tip #2: Don't trip over the flowerpot by the door.

Tip #3: Go to the bathroom before you leave the house; once for forethought, twice if you were ever pregnant, and three times for good measure. Very few weeds are high enough and very few ditches are deep enough to hide you completely should you find yourself a little distressed. This I know.

I'll have to clue in Lila. She might want to try leaving a trail of breadcrumbs, to make it a little easier on the neighbors. Ollie-ollie-ox-in-free.

Of Mice and (WO)Men

For many, many women, the Lord is able to come to them with answers in quiet little ways as they read scriptures with quiet hymns playing in the background, or as they sit by scented candles in the still of an evening and faithfully read their *Ensign* magazines. But there are some of us with whom the Lord must communicate in whatever way He can. And with some of us, He just doesn't have that much to work with.

Here's the upshot of it—one summer I had just sent Levi into the mission field. He was going stateside to Alabama and I was feeling very relieved about that. However, I was missing him. I missed his dry sense of humor. I missed the strength of his quiet but deep testimony. I missed his laughter. I missed his gentle corrections—telling me to quit gossiping, but telling me in the very kindest ways. I missed him so much at odd times during the day I just found myself tearing up. It's a hard thing to let your children go, even when they're going towards something good.

Then, just a few weeks after that son entered the mission home, Will told me he would be leaving for Arizona to take a job there. And, as gently as he could, he let me know that this move might be permanent. I knew this was a good step for him and that he needed to move on with his life. However, Will hadn't met his employer, hadn't seen the ranch where he would be going, and hadn't seen the living arrangements. In short, he was going out into the unknown— taking a leap in the dark. And I would miss him. I would miss his gentleness, his tender ways of caring for me, his hugs. I would miss kissing his neck, because that was as high as I could reach. And I thought my heart was going to break.

Then our realtor called and told us someone had offered to buy our house. This should have been great news; we had the house on the market for several months and were anxious to sell. The problem was we had spent the previous six months looking for a home to move to when our house finally did sell, and hadn't been able to find anything that fit our budget and our family needs. We had looked from one end of the valley to the other and simply couldn't find anything. So now, not only was I worried about Levi and the home he would be making in the mission field, and Will and the home he would be making in Arizona, but now I had to worry about where I would be making a home.

A few weeks went by and still I found no answers. Then one day I went to feed the Sunday dinner scraps to the chickens. I was walking back to the house, still in my Sunday dress, and saw in the grass some distance away a small gray ball. MOUSE! (Barers of disease in our neck of the woods.) Instantly the hunter instinct kicked in. There was no furniture with which to corner it, and if I missed my aim, it could easily hide in the tomato plants; I would have to be accurate on the very first throw. I pulled my shoe off, not even thinking about the run this would cause in my nylons. (Hunters don't think about those things when they catch sight of their prey.) The mouse was just sitting there. If I crept closer I thought I might be able to throw my shoe hard enough to daze it a bit until I could finish him off. So I crept. I didn't even yell when I stepped on the pinecone. Oddly enough, the gray ball didn't run. In fact, it didn't even move. Something was different. When I raised my shoe for the deathblow, I saw that it wasn't a mouse. It was actually a baby bird that had no feathers yet and had obviously fallen from somewhere up in the pine tree. Thank heavens I hadn't thrown the shoe.

I picked up the bird and looked into the tree's branches. There, a few feet above arm's length, was a nest with a very angry mother bird squawking at me. Ah-ha! This was where the baby bird belonged. So I went into the kitchen and brought back a chair to set under the tree. I climbed up on the chair and gently put the baby bird back in its nest. I started to walk back to the house, and a verse of scripture popped into my head, "Are not two sparrows sold for a farthing? and one of them shall not fall on the ground without your Father. But the very hairs of your head are all numbered. Fear ye not therefore, ye are of more value than many sparrows" (Matthew 10:29–31). Then, without any scented candles, without quiet music, and without the still of an evening, I knew. I knew that if a sparrow could not fall from a nest without God noticing and caring, then surely He knew my dilemma. In that quiet, still way, the answer to my prayer came. My Heavenly Father would take care of Levi's nest in Alabama. He would take care of Will's nest in Arizona. And assuredly, He would take care of my nest in my own little Idaho valley.

And He did.

On the Watering of Trees

I knew if I'd toured the old house before we bought the farmstead I'd never sign the papers. It looked like a fixer-upper—more a fixer than an upper. If only we hadn't needed the valuable farm ground it sat on. If only it'd had a few endearing attributes, or quaint peculiarities. If only, if only. With five kids, all the "if onlys" in the world weren't going to house, feed, clothe, and provide braces for them. Only this farm could, so we signed the papers. Then I got up the courage to tour the house.

I started with an I'm-going-to-be-positive-about-this-house-if-it-kills-me attitude. And it nearly did. My husband led me through each room, which reeked of animals and rotting floorboards. The basement smelled of mold and untrapped mice. I was afraid to breathe. When the tour concluded and I had shooed my husband out the door, I slipped out into the backyard, which was overgrown with weeds, and found a scraggly, old pine tree. I leaned against it, the bark poking through my thin shirt, and I cried and cried and cried.

One month and many truckloads of trash later, we were ready to call in the carpenters, plumbers, carpet layers, electricians, and a swarm of others who all charged more than we could afford. We bought five-gallon buckets of paint, light-switch covers, rubber gloves, and ammonia by the case lots. Over the next two months, whenever my energy depleted (and that was often), I found myself again sitting at the base of that sickly pine tree in the backyard, holding handfuls of tissues and trying to cry out my frustrations so I could go back in and tackle the house again.

Toward the end of that summer we finally moved in and slipped back into our comfortable routines as easily as if they'd never been interrupted. The kids started school, the harvest trucks drove by hourly, and we raced to the mailbox each day, just like always. Days went by. Years went by. The pine tree now provided the kids with soldier forts in the spring, tree houses in the summer, and hide-and-seek shelters in the fall. Its green spines gave them needles and tweezers for their pretend medical clinics, and the pinecones gave them ammunition for the magpies. And I occasionally still used the old tree myself.

I cried under that tree when my jars of home-canned peaches wouldn't seal. I cried when the farm cats attacked the baby chickens. I cried when the well pump broke and there was no money to fix it. I cried there when the kids got ear infections. I cried when supper burned. I cried when the freezer unplugged and a hundred pounds of meat spoiled. I cried under it when the bean crop froze, and when rain fell on the mowed hay. I cried under it when we finally held the farm auction, and again when my husband went to look for work in the city. I cried when life was hard, and I cried when living hurt.

I sat under the tree for the last time on moving day. Time to say good-bye. The tree had seen an abundance of change. It had watched my six-year-old child plant flowers upside down. It had seen a new septic line installed and heard all the swear words that went with it. It had watched my husband perch precariously on the roof to paint the eaves. It had seen every load of laundry hung out on the line to dry, a good part of which had landed in its branches. It had seen teenage parties on the back lawn and burnt weiners roasted over glowing coals.

I had decided I wouldn't cry this last time, just recall good memories. The house was in great shape now. The farm was clean and tidy. Someone else held the dreams for this farm now. By now my tears for *this* home had all been shed. More tears would come, I knew, but those tears would be for the next fixer-upper, or new phases of marriage and family—new struggles. On the other hand, that pine tree had been through a great deal with me.

Maybe I could water it just one more time . . .

Tan My Hide
When I'm Dead, Fred

This is my very best nugget of parenting advice—do you have a paper and pen handy to write this down? It's important. Are you ready? *KEEP LOTS OF ASPIRIN HANDY!*

Okay, you probably already knew that one, but I think it's less confusing than this: "We expect something to be a certain way or a person to behave in a certain way and it doesn't happen—so we get upset, bothered, disappointed, and unhappy . . ." A psychologist wrote that. *I* could have written that. I don't need help defining the problem, I need solutions to real-life dilemmas—like boys and basketball.

"He can't quit basketball," I cried, trying not to hyperventilate.

"Yes, he can," Fred reassured me.

"No, he can't."

"Honey" (it sounded more like a term of frustration than endearment), "Homer is seventeen years old. Let him make this decision."

"But it's the wrong one!"

"Let him make it anyway."

"I can't."

"Yes, you can. It may be the wrong decision, but it's not immoral or physically dangerous. He's old enough to decide and be responsible for the consequences."

"Responsible? Have you seen his bedroom lately? And you just remember that agency and accountability are directly tied to responsibility. I'm sure I've heard that during general conference."

"Lynn, let it go."

Let it go? If Homer were responsible I would let it go, but who says he's responsible just because he's now seventeen? He wasn't

responsible two months ago at sixteen. A short fourteen months ago
he was only fifteen years old! Just when did he prove responsible? His
laundry hamper once acquired six towels in two days—is that responsible? He brags about how much he can bench press, but apparently
couldn't lift a finger to turn a light switch off if his life depended on
it. Just yesterday I sent him to the grocery store for almond extract
and he came home without it because he wouldn't ask anyone for
help. I recently asked him to fix the lawn mower and he duct-taped
it—as if I wouldn't notice. He's seventeen. There's a perfectly sane
reason the law doesn't recognize seventeen-year-olds as being mature
enough to sign apartment contracts or make automobile purchases.
There's a reason why even the army doesn't want them; they haven't
even started to become "all they can be." They're irresponsible. And
that's precisely why they need their moms' help.

Not that I didn't try to teach him. I'm sure I covered the you-
don't-quit-in-the-middle-of-something lesson. Isn't that why we
suffered through the trombone? It came right after the don't-pick-
your-teeth-in-public lesson and the lesson on which table fork to use.
But no, his dad laughed and taught him how to hang his spoon on
the end of his nose instead. Guess which lesson he remembered best?

I taught him how to neatly make his bed; his dad taught him to
throw the bedspread over the whole lumpy mess. I taught him to
drink milk without getting a white mustache; his dad taught him to
suction his milk glass to his cheeks. I taught him to hold his fork
properly; his dad taught him to spit watermelon seeds without drib-
bling down his chin.

That's it! It's all his dad's fault. I taught him to say please and
thank you. His dad taught him to make root beer foam out his nose.
I signed him up for piano lessons. His dad taught him to sing "Tan
My Hide When I'm Dead, Fred." I taught him to read classics, but he
reads Westerns like his dad. I bought him a microscope, and his dad
bought him a motorcycle helmet.

Didn't I teach him to change his underwear and socks and not to
sit too close to the TV? I tried. I potty-trained him to use the real
toilet; his dad taught him to write his name in the weeds out back.
Now look what this all has led to—he's quitting basketball. AND IT
WILL BE HIS DAD'S FAULT.

"He's basically a good kid, Lynn. Give him some space. He'll turn out alright."

"Hmmm." I was suspicious. "Just exactly what is your definition of 'alright'?"

"He'll have my sense of humor and your ulcers."

"Now you're making fun of me. See, dear, that's the problem. Sometimes you have to be serious."

"And sometimes you have to lighten up."

"Sometimes you have to hold the line."

"But sometimes you have to bend it a little."

"So you'd have Homer quit basketball, and continue to believe spitting watermelon seeds is an art form and sticking a spoon to his nose is a talent?"

"Is that such a bad thing?"

Dare I answer that? "So if I say black, you'll say . . ."

"White."

"That's it! That's the problem."

"What's the problem?"

"HE'S JUST LIKE YOU!"

"Yeah? Then just think how good he'll marry."

Now I'm confused. Did I win? I went back to the professional's quote and read on: "We expect something to be a certain way or a person to behave in a certain way and it doesn't happen—so we get upset, bothered, disappointed, and unhappy . . . In no way am I suggesting that you eliminate your preferences or all of your expectations. Certainly there will be times when you will want to insist on certain things or demand certain standards of behavior, and that's fine. But lessening your expectations is *not* the same thing as lowering your standards! It's entirely possible to have very high standards, yet still keep your perspective about your own expectations" (*Don't Sweat the Small Stuff with Your Family*, Richard Carlson, PhD).

And still I'm confused. High standards are not difficult to set. It's that whole hyperventilating "perspective about [my] own expectations" behavior that requires a bottle of aspirin. Maybe it's just a parenting manual that I need. I'm pretty sure one exists. One morning my son Levi, who was about ten years old at the time, said, "Mom, what's for breakfast?" I didn't answer right away because, quite frankly, I had no idea what I was fixing. Levi then whispered, "Say, 'French toast.' That's your line."

See? He knows the script, but someone forgot to teach it to me! When it comes to parenting I simply have no clue what I'm doing. It's trial and error. And then error again. I have five grown children now, and I only feel smarter today than the day they were born, because now I *know* that I don't know a thing. And the kids also know that I don't know a thing.

I keep telling myself, "It's the parents who can't admit they're crazy who are scary. I can admit it. Therefore, I'm not nearly as crazy or scary as other parents."

Hmm. On paper that sounds like a really pathetic circle. Is it any wonder my son quit basketball? Is it any wonder I argue in circles? Is it any wonder I need aspirin?

When Push Comes to Shove

I'm so mad I could spit. I overheard a woman say that behind every award-winning child is a pushy mother. That touched a nerve with me. My children have won an award or two, and not one of them was pushed. They were negotiated. There is a difference.

Negotiations are delicate. When negotiations are done right, the subject won't even know he's been had. That's not pushiness; it's effectiveness. And there's a place for effective mothers, wives, and women in this world. Especially if one has mice.

This fall the mice have been waging war in my kitchen. They have breached the unwritten limit of four per autumn, and someone has to enforce the rules. Is a noodly wife going to do it? I think not. She'll nag the husband to buy bait, and set traps, and bang the really dumb ones over the head with a shoe. (Not that I'd know.) The husband will then become annoyed and perhaps defensive (not that I'd know), and the mice will go right on dropping their doots whithersoever they please.

But an *effective* wife cuts a deal. She tells the husband that he must forthwith dispatch to the shop for a piece of board to cover the holes, and in return she will not require his help to install it. This is effective. The husband thinks he's getting away with the better end of the bargain and off he goes, thinking he's the most helpful husband in the world. Then, rather than bargain for his labor in actually putting up the board, the effective wife will begin the repair on her own—with all of her vast expertise in power saws, wood adhesives, chisels, and drill bits, and using Legos and an old doorknob for a clamp. This makes the husband nervous, and he becomes very anxious to correct her ineptness (not that I'd know). Thus she has "engaged" his help without so much as a hint of a threat. Now, she'll get the job done, and I challenge anyone to find pushiness in that situation.

Another example: It's Tuesday night and my eighteen-year-old, the should-know-better-than-to-procrastinate son, has an essay due tomorrow. He wants his paper typed. He wants me to do it. I say no. He says please. I say absolutely not. He goes to find a radio to "help" him. He types slowly and gets that glazed-over stare while the computer monitor glows into his eyes. He takes a break (from what I'm not sure). He gets a snack. Two hours later he has three pathetic paragraphs. It's now 10:00 P.M. and I'm on my way to bed. He can see this is going to be a long night. As I kiss him good night, I tell him this is his own fault, as I reminded him of the due date on Sunday. I reminded him again Monday. I remind him now that I don't feel sorry for him one bit. I'm tempted to be smug, but I restrain myself—in the interest of effectiveness. I yawn and wave. And as I head for the bedroom, he slowly (very reluctantly) says, "Okay, what do you want?"

Please note, I—did—not—push—one—inch—of—the—way, but there I have it, a son begging at the bargaining table. And the best part is, he's pleading for mercy and only I can grant it. Is this too good to miss?

I say, "Homer, I'll type your paper on these conditions: One, you make two phone calls tonight as part of research for your term paper that's due at the end of the term; two, you must participate with the family on Monday night for a highway cleanup project, AND BE HAPPY ABOUT IT; and three, you must help your brother with his Scout project on Saturday."

Because he is a teenager and he thinks this is a game, he tries to counteroffer: "Two phone calls for the term paper, forget highway cleanup, and don't I get credit for already helping on other Scout projects?"

I simply yawn and turn for the bedroom.

"Okay, okay," he says. "Two phone calls, the Scout badge, but no highway cleanup."

No deal; I keep walking. I put on my pajamas. Then I hear a knock at the bedroom door. "Okay, I guess I could help with the family project, too."

"And . . ." I prompt. Long pause.

"Oh, alright. I won't call anybody a moron." And a contract is born. It's a beautiful thing.

Negotiating is how kids remember to empty their pockets before putting their pants in the laundry, and clear their dishes from the table, and replace the empty toilet paper roll. Negotiating is how husbands remember to pick up milk at the supermarket and learn to overlook those itty-bitty overdrafts. Those things are a piece of cake, but you have to start somewhere. For the novice, it's nice to begin with small things, then work up to acquiring snow tires, and lobster dinners, and a trash compactor. (Not that I'd know.)

The Whole
Family-Bonding Thing

One day I asked Rachel (eleven) if I could have one of her potato chips. She took one out of the bag, licked it, and then handed it to me. Now she could have said yes, but she would have meant no. However, the licking came through loud and clear. No subtleties there.

As Jenny (eighteen) prepared for college and her first real adventures away from home, I sometimes wondered if she would experience homesickness. She answered this for me by coming into the kitchen and announcing, "When I move out I'm going to have my OWN toothbrush!" I think we cleared up that issue.

The boys are another species altogether. Whenever Homer (seventeen) starts a sentence with, "Mom, I love you," it's usually followed by, "Can I use the pickup tonight?" or, "Can I go hunting now?" Does he think I don't get it? Does he think he's the first one to invent a snow job? He and I need to work on communication. I think I'll start by wearing a sign that says HOMER, I'M NOT STUPID.

Levi and I have had communication problems since he was little. Remember the french-toast-for-breakfast story a couple of chapters ago? Well, when Levi was thirteen our communication problem still existed. The kids at school had figured out the school pay phone a long time ago: for five cents you could hear the other person talk, for ten cents they can hear you talk, and for twenty-five cents you can hear each other. But when Levi wanted to call home, he'd usually find a nickel in the hallway somewhere, deposit it into the phone, and then just yell really loud, hoping I would hear him anyway—which I couldn't. So whenever the phone rang and no one seemed to be on the other end of the line, I just shouted, "Dang it, Levi, put a dime in!"

And then there's Will (fourteen). He caught a touchdown pass in football season, shot his first deer, grew three inches, and had a drop in his voice. I guess for a fourteen-year-old boy it just doesn't get any better than this. Now that he's out of the Tonka-truck stage, our communication seems to be basically limited to: "How many times do I have to trip over your shoes before you put them away?"

To this he responds, "Is there anything good to eat?"

Then I ask, "So how did school go today?"

And he responds, "Is there anything good to eat?"

Communications with my boys are further hampered because they are totally disgusted that I can't keep the teams straight in the NFL, NBA, EPA, or FBI. I can't remember from one day to the next, let alone one season to the next, if it's the Hawks, Orioles, or Cardinals that play hockey. Why in the world hasn't someone passed a law keeping all the dang bird mascots in one sport?

I tried valiantly to resolve these communication problems with all the kids, so we could do the bonding thing. That's when we put the Dishwashing Plan into effect. They could take turns doing dishes with me and drill me on the Jaguars, Panthers, and other pertinent adolescent information, and I would try very hard to be a good sport (no pun intended; give me a little credit, if I had intended one it would have been better than that).

Gradually, over bacon grease and soap suds, Rachel learned that spaghetti noodles aren't sweepable, Will learned that dishrags don't go in the dishwasher, and Levi learned that I'm bound to win in a dish-towel-snapping fight because my arms are longer. I inventoried Homer's school's locker-room gossip, which of Jenny's friends were fighting over which boys, and who had head lice at school that month. Sometimes we reviewed spelling words, or history questions, or learned a very old jump-rope rhyme. We even sang off-key to a warped version of "On Top of Old Smokey."

The dishwashing lasted several months, but then suddenly the gig was up. Will came in one night and said, "Since it's my night to do dishes, could you fix something easy with not too many dishes? I don't feel like bonding."

I wish I had worried about the bonding thing long ago before that boat had sailed. I guess I should have started when they were younger. Or at least when *I* was younger.

Cowboy Up

We have all been given gifts of the Spirit, like faith, testimony, tongues, discernment, knowledge, and wisdom. President George Q. Cannon gave a discourse in 1894 in which he said, "How many of you . . . are seeking for these gifts that God has promised to bestow? . . . If any of us are imperfect, it is our duty to pray for the gift that will make us perfect." Well, when we lined up in heaven for gifts, I obviously wasn't wise enough to get in the wisdom line.

One day Fred and I were at Will's football game. Will made a great catch, then was tackled and lay groaning on the field. The officials stopped the game, and the coaches and trainers ran onto the field. The other players stood around watching curiously, secretly hoping, I assume, they could get him off the field to continue their drive.

But where was Mom? Where was the legal guardian? The signer of athletic injury waivers? The insurance-premium payer? In the stupid grandstands—wondering if her six-foot-two-inch boy needed a kiss to make him feel better, or a stretcher. I have never fantasized about being a doctor or a nurse, and I only pretended to know what first-aid class was about, so what was I supposed to do? Even if I knew what to do, was I supposed to do it from the grandstands? Should I have run onto the field? Should I have held my little boy's hand in front of those great big linemen—who just smeared him, thank you very much—and tell him everything was all right? Should I have let him be carried off a hero? Or, should I have just grabbed a megaphone and yelled, "Buck up!"

I think I am what they might call "medically challenged." Over the years I have never placed a poultice, never ground herbs or administered cardiopulmonary resuscitation. If an injury requires anything more than aspirin, then my suggestion to the patient is to take a long nap. I don't recall much of anything that a kiss and a damp washrag couldn't cure. Well, okay, maybe there *was* that other time . . .

Levi, at about age eleven, was practicing dunking a basketball from the picnic table. The picnic table was essential because he was only about four feet tall at the time. On one attempt he fell off balance and put out his hand to break the fall. *(Break* is an especially appropriate word here.) Well, I reasoned, haven't we all banged our wrist a little playing Red Rover with the Cub Scouts? Twisted it when trying to stuff one more box in the hall closet and the whole kit and caboodle fell on top of us? Bruised it when falling over a school backpack in the living room? Or stressed it launching bottle rockets at pack meeting? But did *we* go to the doctor?

Of course not. Most of us were overdrawn in our checking accounts for the month as it was, so we just bucked up. We cradled it, Ace-wrapped it, took aspirin, and were glad we had an excuse to get out of washing dishes. Why then (when little boys play tackle football with no pads whatsoever, walk fence rails, jump off the roof when fetching Annie-Aye-Over balls, and build bicycle jumps out of 2x4s) should a little old fall during a jump from a picnic table be such a big deal? When Levi came in and said his wrist hurt, I made him hold it still, Ace-wrapped it, gave him some aspirin, and kissed him better. Period.

I don't know—perhaps his complaints of throbbing, and the whining at night were hints that this was more serious. But, it was a judgment call. If you're a parent, you understand a missed diagnosis. Levi didn't. It could be that he was remembering the ankle incident— the *broken* ankle incident. I missed the diagnosis then, too, but I think he should still have forgiven me—it wasn't as bad as his father's heart attack.

We can laugh about the heart attack now that everything is fine. But when Fred came in early one Tuesday morning to tell me his shoulder and arm hurt, that he had chest pressure, and he was sweating profusely, not once did I add it up to heart problems (you may need to refer to my initial statement about only pretending to understand first-aid classes). I told him he should expect as much for being out of shape and playing a rigorous game of golf the day before. Really, who hasn't done that before? Aches and pains are common enough. It hurts, we moan—but do we really need all those X-rays and doctors' assistants and doctors coming in to tell us we're overreacting? Of course not—we have brains. We know it's going to be painful. Such is life. Toughen up. Buck up. Cowboy up.

Fred proceeded to lie on the floor and ask me to *adjust* his back— as I had done from time to time with all my medical training. So I proceeded to jump up and down on his back.

He had the nerve, then, to still not feel better. He wanted me to call for some help. I argued. After all, he had an appointment with the doctor that afternoon for a checkup. Couldn't he just bite the bullet until then? No, he said, he couldn't. Fine, then.

With some pretense at cooperation, I dialed the doctor's number so that the doctor, who has more authority than a little old wife, could back me up and tell him to toughen up; he'd see him later at his scheduled appointment. It almost worked—except for that whole heart attack thing.

For a week Fred lay in intensive care with a look on his face that said, "I was hurting and trying to get help, and having a heart attack, and you wanted me to COWBOY UP? How heartless is that?"

That's all water under the bridge now, at least in my book. In the meantime, my son lay groaning on a football field. What was I supposed to do? I don't have King Solomon's wisdom, although I suppose I could have offered to split his knee in half with a sword to see if he would jump up or not. Fortunately, he didn't have to rely on my wisdom. His coach and his dad were there to give him a priesthood blessing.

Since my sword for splitting things in half is usually in my *other purse*—never handy when I need it—perhaps I'd better take President Cannon's advice and pray for that wisdom gift. In the meantime, if my kids are going to live to be adults, I guess I have to count on the priesthood to pick up the slack.

Niagara Falls and Mount Rushmore in Southern Idaho

I think the Lord may have intended to write, THOU SHALT HAVE FAMILY REUNIONS on those tablets of stone, but my theory is that He got to laughing so hard over that one that He finally just left it off.

I can't even begin to count the days that have started with, "Mom, Levi hid the TV remote and won't tell me where it is," or, "Mom, Rachel keeps throwing her stuff on my side of the room. Make her stop!" One day, Rachel informed me that her friend's family was going to Hawaii for Thanksgiving. "Can you believe that?" she asked. "The whole family!" She thought about this not with envy but—as a true redhead should—immediately added, "I'll have to tell Brad that *our* family can fight just as well in Idaho as in Hawaii!" And she's right. The whole fam-damily can ruin a vacation right here in the home state. We've had practice.

I envy families who bicycle together, camp together, or who can even agree to see the same movie together. But when I think down the road to planning family reunions, I sometimes wonder if my family will even be on speaking terms by then.

My children—other than having the same blue eyes, similar complexions, and the same incredible and wonderfully talented mother—don't seem to have anything in common at all. Then I remember—cars. They do have cars in common. Or more accurately, car *trouble*. This is an unending source of embarrassment. When we sit down to have a meal together, I can ignite even the most introverted of our children by simply asking, "Who had car trouble today?" And the I-can-top-that race is on.

One suppertime, Jenny said, "Well, the bank manager at work had to push-start my car three times in a row today."

Fred asked, "Three times? It wouldn't start the first two times he tried?"

Jenny (the high school valedictorian) blushingly admitted, "Well, no one told me I was supposed to let the clutch out the first two times." Then she added, "I parked it by the shop for you to fix, Dad."

Another suppertime, Will, who didn't yet have a driver's license, said, "Dad, I think the axle in the Honda broke."

"You *think?*"

"Well, I took it out in the pasture to irrigate (*He couldn't walk thirty yards?!*) and it got stuck bouncing over the corrugates. Now it won't do anything."

Fred, looking a little harried, said, "Well, pull it over by the shop and I'll take a look at it."

But Homer said, "It'll have to wait, Will. Dad promised he'd fix my pickup yesterday."

Then I rather stupidly asked, "Do I want to know what it's going to cost to fix the pickup?"

Homer: "No."

Trying to soothe my feathers before they even became ruffled, Fred asked, "Lynn, is the Tempo running okay?" Wrong question. *Way* wrong question.

"No. Do you want me to list things by noise level or color of warning light? But you know, that young man at the garage knows me by name now and he even helped me pick out wallpaper the other day. He thinks peach is a good color for the kitchen. What do you think?"

"Just pull the car over by the shop—if there's room," Fred said resignedly.

And then one evening, Rachel or Levi (far under driving age, but they used to drive an old beater pickup down the lane to catch the school bus) complained, "The white pickup makes a funny noise when I turn the wheel."

And the first simple answer in weeks finally came to Fred, almost instinctively. "Then turn the radio up!"

For the most part I've given Fred the silent treatment over nearly every run-down, run-over, can't-pass-'em-up vehicle he's bought. It's the fact that he's so proud of them that really irritates me. I did eventually forgive him for one, the International pickup he bought when Homer was sixteen years old. It was a gas guzzler and only pushed fifty miles per hour if there was a stiff tailwind. It wasn't much better than a bicycle, but it had wheels—all four, even. I have since come to the conclusion that every sixteen-year-old boy should have an old pickup that makes him feel important, but keeps his bank account empty enough that he will be humble and dependent on his folks.

I can't tell you all the good that has come from the old egg crates we've driven. No, really—I can't tell you. Fred and the boys claim they have spent endless hours in the shop replacing one worn-out part after another. I have spent endless hours in the house wondering what it was they really did out there. One day the boys came in and bragged, "Yeah, we really bonded tonight. Dad showed us how to hot-wire a pickup."

Hot-wire a pickup? Gee, I was afraid they were doing nothing constructive. Our family might get to go on vacation after all; the nearest state penitentiary is only two hours away.

"Why in blazes would you teach our boys how to hot-wire a pickup?" I asked Fred.

"It might come in handy someday."

"For crying out loud—when? When they need a getaway car?"

Is it any wonder that I sometimes worry how our family memories will turn out? When other families reminisce about Yellowstone Park, we'll fondly remember the oil geyser from "old Bob," which could be counted on to erupt every fifteen minutes or fifteen miles, whichever came first. When other families remember the emerald mineral pools of Wyoming, we'll remember the beautiful rainbow in the antifreeze pool under "old Blue." Other family reunions might include games and picnics and water slides; ours will include mufflers, brakes, transmission fluid, and a tour of the auto salvage yard. When other families recall the roar of Niagara Falls, we'll declare that nobody but nobody had a backfire louder than "The Green Machine." Other families will say, "We can't sell the station wagon—it took us all the way to Mount Rushmore." And we'll say, "You can't sell the Monte Carlo—I just figured out how to roll down the window with the screwdriver. And even though she rides like a boat, I'm not getting seasick anymore."

I shouldn't worry. When I'm old and the kids all come home for a family reunion, I'm positive they will be speaking to each other after all. They'll still be arguing about who had the worst car.

The Dating Game

One year Homer and his friends decided to bring their dates to our house for an expensive-looking but cheap-costing dinner (largely because good old Mom doesn't charge sales tax or gratuity). For two days our home was in pandemonium. I scrounged through closets and storage boxes and even in the bottom of the fabric bag to look for an Italian-lace tablecloth that I'm sure I once owned. Nothing. Then I tried to find matching pieces of silverware. The good news is that I found the soup ladle in the tulip bulb box (it's the obvious, bulb-sized choice for spring planting), and the butter knife in the pencil box (I guess it works as the letter opener). The bad news is, it was downhill from there.

My wedding was twenty years and five kids ago, and every piece of china I have has a chip in it, except, of course, the one emblazoned with stove-burner rings. If we only had matching plates to worry about, it would have been no big deal, but I didn't have any nice serving dishes, either. The serving dishes I used to own were taken to one funeral dinner too many (I think it was two), and the dishes never made it home again. The poor, late gravy boat sank as a submarine in the tub (undoubtedly that would have been while Fred was supposed to be babysitting). In fact, when Aunt Roene and Uncle Everett visited, I had to serve the salad in a margarine tub, the mashed potatoes in a disposable pie tin, and the gravy from the plastic water pitcher that still had Easter-egg-dye stains in it. So, you see, a prom dinner was certainly a stretch for my meager capacity. It was just a good thing Christine (my sister) lived close by. She had a full china cabinet, a taste for fancy dinners, and only two kids—she had only lost two teacups out of her set. So I called her and she lent me her china with the dainty rose-colored ring of flowers around the rims, which would have been just dandy if I'd had a tablecloth, napkins, and salt shakers to match. However, Christine (afraid I'd try to put the condiments in pint-sized mason jars) loaned me serving dishes, napkins, a tablecloth, and the whole shebang. Bless her heart. The table looked great—thus far.

The dish dilemma turned out to be minor compared to the chair dilemma. At one time, I believe, we had six chairs in the dining set. We now have two chairs that were stripped for refinishing, and two chairs that were not stripped because the kids kept rocking on the chair legs and I figured they'd fall apart long before I got around to varnishing them. Other options were a homemade bench (which hurts any hiney over 50 pounds) and folding chairs. Obviously, I couldn't consider letting company use the folding chairs because PROPERTY OF HOLLISTER LDS CHURCH is written across the backs of them in black permanent marker, and then it would be known I didn't return them. By process of elimination, the two stripped chairs and the two un-stripped chairs won. My girls, bless their hearts, told me not to worry about it, because once the prom-goers sat down they wouldn't notice anyway.

For a table centerpiece, I took two vases of dried roses and basi-cally tried to rearrange them together to make one passable arrange-ment. But there's just something about dead flowers in the middle of a table that makes it look sort of—I don't know . . . dead? I might have settled for dandelions, but they hadn't bloomed yet. In the end we decided dead flowers would have to suffice.

My last preparation was rounding up the family for the obligatory Company Manners Lecture. This was the part where I told the younger, non-dating kids not to walk through the house in their underwear, to keep their feet off the couch, not to scratch themselves anywhere at all, to keep their noses off the window when the dates are coming up the walk, and finally, to leave the bathroom door closed until the flush is *completely finished.* The difference, this time, was that as well as giving this lecture to the kids, I had to give it to their father. Bless his heart.

It's all over now. The dinner was lovely. The girls in their dresses, the boys in their tuxes, the flowers and corsages, the good-natured picture posing—it was all wonderful. The kids were sort of nervous, so I don't suppose anyone will remember the mismatched chairs. And no one will care that the napkins weren't fluted. At 11:45 P.M., all that was left was to wait up for the last child to come home, tuck them all into bed, and bless their hearts, every one.

One Fish, Two Fish

I'm not sure we're ever supposed to figure out parenting, and we certainly shouldn't expect to be good at it. It's pretty darn confusing, whether you're just beginning parenting (and your two-year-old shouts, "No Mommy, no Mommy, no spank!" all the way through the grocery store) or whether you're trying to teach responsibility to teenagers.

One time Levi needed to take a fish to his speech class because he was giving a speech on how to gut a fish. When he came home and told me this four days beforehand, I said, "Great. Do you know how to gut a fish?"

"Well, I think so." I took this to mean, "It doesn't matter, I know I'll get an A if I just take a slimy fish to class to demonstrate. It's a great visual."

I thought we ought to clear this up. "Great, and where are you going to get this fish? Have you forgotten this is February, in Idaho? You'd better start fishing now." What was he thinking? Well, actually I know what he was thinking—he was thinking his mom or dad would bail him out. Fred, however, had just flown to Las Vegas for a conference and would be gone for the rest of the week, so it was left to me to do the enabling. It's one thing I'm really good at.

I tried to do the right thing first. I told him to get some papier-mâché and make a fish, with guts and all. He thought that idea was *stupid*. I told him to call Pat Callen—Pat always ice-fishes in the winter. Levi said he didn't have a clue who Pat Callen was and felt, ah—*stupid*. I told him to draw pictures and make diagrams. He thought that was—um, what's the word here . . . *stupid?* And besides, it wouldn't get him the A he knew he deserved. I left it at that for two days, and he started leaving me little sticky notes all around the house that said, "Mom, think fish . . ."

Finally, because Levi is so endearing and hard to resist, I did the honorable thing and begged a stinky, slimy specimen off a local fish factory—at which time I felt really—ummm . . . I don't know—oh yeah . . . *STUPID.*

In contrast, I had no trouble holding the parental line with Homer. Homer used to make me so blooming mad I even derived some pleasure out of not wavering. I don't generally curse, but if I ever did it usually was connected to Homer in some way. Levi was a much harder child to raise because he's always so darned undemanding and kind; it's so easy to do the WRONG thing *for* him.

Speaking of enabling, one Sunday Rachel spent the day with Jenny and her husband Ed. By evening Rachel and Ed were tired of each other and fighting. Rachel really loves to goad him and just generally push his buttons. Ed plays into it perfectly. In fairness, I would have to say it really isn't a fair fight; Rachel obviously has the upper hand. Ed is much too easy.

Ed kept saying, "Mom, aren't you going to do something about this?" I guess he thought that was a mother-in-law's job, to protect him and make Rachel quit annoying him, so I did the motherly thing. I told him, "Ed, you deserve each other. Quit whining."

Finally, Jenny got up and sat between them on the couch. I said, "Honey, don't rescue him. Let them kill each other. Ed's got to learn to fight for himself." But bless her heart, she couldn't help herself.

My conclusion is that, unfortunately, I have raised Jenny to be an enabler, like me, and Levi to be too dependent, although I don't think I'll have any trouble raising Ed.

The Chihuahua Factor

"Don't go to bed mad." How many of us have heard that advice? Had I always taken this advice I would have died from lack of sleep long ago. Some people are just Chihuahuas (always barking and worked up about something—usually something inconsequential), and *I is one*. It's just one of those little flaws of my character.

"Has anybody seen my book lately?" I asked.

"Which one?" questioned one of my boys. "*The House of Seven Gables* novel in the van?" He wrinkled his nose. "The Relief Society book in the bathroom?" He rolled his eyes. "Or the fourth-grade reader on the bed stand?"

"None of the above, Mr. Smarty Pants. I need the gold-mining history book."

He was laying back against a pillow playing a video game, thumbs bobbing automatically up and down. My obvious impatience didn't break his stride. "Why do you read that boring stuff anyway?" he added.

Boring? How dare he call it boring? "It's not boring. It's research. It's informative, and I like it. It's . . . it's . . . why aren't you helping me look?" As I pulled books off the pine shelves, the stack tipped over, sliding onto his stomach, but his thumbs never skipped a beat.

"It's a snoozer," he insisted.

"Well, only to people under forty."

"So basically half the population?" That grin of his appeared, the one that makes me want to bite his pant leg like a Chihuahua—not to inflict harm really, just to worry it a bit.

"Why do I argue with you? I'm the adult here," I mumbled. Then I wondered if I should have to keep reminding myself of that.

"Mom, admit it. If you had to take out a personals ad you'd have to say, 'White female, forty-something going on sixty. Looking for someone to visit museums with.'"

"You're not funny."

"I'm not finished. 'Likes *The History of Idaho* book for fourth-graders—"

"I should have written that."

"And still watches for Neil Diamond concerts. Like that's ever gonna happen."

"Still not funny."

"But true."

"Yes, truly unfunny."

"You need a life, Mom."

This teenager engrossed in his video game says *I* need a life? The obvious irony would escape him. "And in your opinion a 'life' would include what?"

"Parties."

"I went to a baccalaureate planning meeting last week."

"Party on, Mom. What about friends?"

"Exchanging Christmas cards doesn't count?" The books were now stacked high and a two-foot wall of dusty paperbacks lay between us.

"Fortune."

"There's thirty-five cents right here!" I held up some forgotten coins from the bottom of the bookshelf.

"Fame," he added.

"My name was in the ward bulletin yesterday—twice if you count the library overdue list."

"You're missing the point."

"No, I got it loud and clear." Now what was it I was looking for? "Throw me that dust rag." His thumbs stopped long enough to flick a towel in my direction. "I just don't happen to agree with your point."

He calmly blacked out the TV tube and got up to leave.

"Hey, where are you going? You can't leave until I say you can. And you certainly can't leave the argument when I'm winning."

"You're not winning, Mom. You're just annoying."

"AH-HAH!" I triumphantly flicked the dishtowel, snapping it at his calves. "You left the issue first and sank to personal attacks. Guess what that means?"

"I let you win?" He was still so dang calm. I hate that.

"LET me? I don't THINK so. I won fair and square. It's game, set, and match!"

"Not quite. You *would* have won *if* you hadn't taken the bait to begin with, *Mother*."

If I won, then I'm wondering why I'm so uptight and he's so relaxed. Why is it I have these debates in the first place, when I always seem to lose them? Once again I'll lie in bed at night, not being able to sleep, rewording that conversation over and over again in my head, trying for a different outcome.

The truth of it is, I don't even need a face-to-face confrontation. I can get worked up simply over e-mail. When Rachel was thirteen, she stayed with her aunt for a week in the summer, and sent me this e-mail:

Mom,

aunt jane said I had to write you. Not that I didnt want to but . . . any way. How are things at home? Are the turkeys still alive? Have you gotten a letter from homer? Today we went swimming. We had a lot of fun. Right now cali is in japan, the boys are at EFY, and aunt jane and uncle calvin went on a date, so that leaves ande and I alone at home. PARTY!!!!!! right now we have TONS of hot hot GUYS here!!!!! not!!! there's only about 6, three for me & three for ande. Don't worry nothings happening but dancing. Do you know how hard it is to dance with three guys at once? Its pretty hard!!! (I should know) well gotta go were gonna watch "scary movie" at the theature, you know, the one thats rated "R"? One of my men knows how to hot-wire a car, then were gonna sneek in. Love ya!!!!!!

Your favorite daughter
(Rachel, ya know, the cute one)

And out came my Chihuahua:

> Dear Rachel,
>
> I thought I better write back, though I really didn't want to, but anyway . . . I forgot all about the turkeys. I'm sure they're missing you throwing corn at them through the chicken wire and spraying them with the hose. Will is at work. Dad is at work, so today it's PAR-TY!!! I thought maybe I'd run around the house in my underwear, then watch Donnie and Marie and eat potato chips and dip. Then I'll invite a bunch of ladies over to gab about our DAUGHTERS and, well, you know how I exaggerate things . . . hope you don't mind. Then I'll probably really let my hair hang down and go to the library and TALK REALLY LOUD. They might even kick me out, but, hey, I feel like taking risks today.
>
> So enjoy your HOT GUYS and your NIGHTMARE MOVIE for which you have NO PARENTAL PERMISSION, and I hope the HOT MEN get thrown in jail for hot-wiring the car and sneaking in.
>
> Tah, tah.
>
> Your favorite Mother
> (Ya know, the embarrassing one)

Is there a point here, then? Some little timeless conclusion or lesson learned that will wrest this nasty little habit from my character? I'm sure I could come up with it, if I could just quit chewing on things long enough to get a really good night's rest!

College Lessons

It's time to get another son ready for college and to live on his own. I've done this before. You'd think I'd know what I'm doing, but no—this is cram summer. This summer I will have to fit in all the lessons I have heretofore neglected to teach him. I already taught the do-not-walk-through-the-house-in-your-underwear lesson, the keep-your-feet-off-the-couch lesson, the keep-your-nose-off-the-window-and-your-tongue-off-frozen-metal lesson, and the say-your-prayers-every-night lesson. Yes, those are covered. What I have yet to teach this summer is how to make gravy, how to not mix jeans and white shirts in the same laundry load, how to not eat everything in the fridge until he's checked for mold, and how to open an apartment door with a credit card when he loses his keys—or maybe he should figure that one out the way the rest of us did, when it is one o'clock in the morning, thirty degrees below zero, everyone else has gone home for the holidays, and the car keys are locked in the apartment.

This particular child who is leaving in the fall is eighteen and a good student. You'd think he'd know how to fill out a class registration form and a housing agreement and read a campus map. He hasn't, can't, and doesn't. I get tension headaches over this, but it doesn't seem to concern him in the least. This lackadaisical attitude is one of the fundamental differences between boys and girls. When a group of Mia Maids goes camping, they plan for months in advance. They come up with a theme, little gifts to exchange, decorations, and a thought for each day. They pack cots and bedrolls, air mattresses, tents, Dutch ovens, solar showers, crafts, and plan activities galore.

When the Boy Scouts go camping, they take a package of hot dogs, a bedroll, a pocketknife for entertainment, and wonder what all the fuss is about.

This is precisely why I have trouble getting my boys ready to live on their own. They think they are ready. Ha! We discussed a simple thing like bedding the other day. I asked how many blankets he was going to want.

He said, "I think I'll just take a sleeping bag."

"WHAT?"

"Then I won't have to worry about washing sheets."

"Oh, good thinking. And how are you going to WASH THE SLEEPING BAG?" I truly wish I were one of those moms who could just let it go—just let her eighteen-year-old son make his own decisions about a simple thing like bedding. In the whole blue cosmos, how important is bedding?

But, but, but I can't let it go. Doesn't he know that you can only spread your feet apart something like fourteen inches in a bedroll? Doesn't he know that bedrolls are made for cold mountain climates and he'd sweat to death sleeping in one in an apartment? Doesn't he know that's just *not how it's done?*

I'll win, of course, if you can call it winning. His lack of planning will drive me nuts and I'll go to Wally-World and buy him some cheap sheets and a cheaper blanket and then, and then, and then . . . I'll be the one sleeping better at night. Then once he's been gone for a few months, I'll look back on the whole thing and decide he was right—he really only needed a package of hot dogs, a bedroll, and a pocketknife. What was I thinking?

SEASON III

As Sisters in Zion,
We'll All Whine Together

Back-door Entrance

My back porch looks like the burnt-orange mudroom from you-know-where. It's ugly and smelly and disgusting. The thing that really fries my bacon, though, is how many guests keep coming to the porch entry to make social calls.

I know that in the city it is usual and customary for a guest to use the front door (the one with the wreath hanging on it). But out here in the country, my Relief Society wreath keeps blowing away. And I have yet to greet company at my front door. Why is it so different in rural, mud-swallows-nesting-on-the-porch-light America? Why can't people use my *front* door? What is their problem?

My back door does not say, "Welcome Friends." Just because the wind can come right through doesn't mean they can. Do they have any idea what sights and smells await them behind this door? The box of shriveled apples; the scattered scripture markers, old tithing slips, pens, and puzzles that someone dumped from my Sunday bag; the pieces of shower pipe; the mud-packed boots; the backpacks; the fabric-softener sheets that fall off the shelf every time someone slams the door; the paint cans; the laundry baskets; and the kawhumping washing machine—it's crowded out there. This is the place where we bring in sick animals from time to time. This is the place with orange linoleum left over from the '70s that I can't afford to replace because it wears like steel wool. This is the low spot in the house, and on the days when the sewer backs up (due to improper venting) it could bring Rosie the Riveter to her knees. This is the place covered in lint from the hole in my dryer vent.

What makes neighbors think this is a side of me I want them to see? These things do not say, "Come on in, I've been waiting for a moment like this to expose you to my worst side."

To all neighbors everywhere, I say, "Stop it. Now. Do not use my back door. Even if I know you very, very well, I do not want to be so intimate with you that you know I wear queen-sized pantyhose with a run in the top, which just happen to be hanging up to dry."

From now on, I have decided that anyone wishing to use my back door must complete the following application:

APPLICATION FOR PERMISSION TO USE MY BACK DOOR

1) Name_____ Date of Birth _____
2) Height _____ Weight_____ Girth _____
3) I.Q. _____ General Reaction Time (in milliseconds)_____
4) Family Doctor _____ Doctor's Beeper # _____
5) Allergies? _____
6) Do you have a sensitive nose? _____
7) Do you have heart problems, or does your stomach turn easily? ____
8) Is your tetanus shot current? _____
9) When you have a secret, just how many people do you take into "confidence?" And would any of them be living within, say, 3,000 miles? If the answer is yes, please list these friends on a separate sheet of paper with names and addresses so I can invite them to my next 100 kitchenware parties.
10) Do your shoes have good traction? _____
11) Is your bishop young? Yes_____ No _____ Does he have lots of counseling time available? Yes _____ No _____
12) In 50 words or fewer, what does **ringworm** mean to you?

   _____

   _____

13) In 50 words or less, what does **pinkeye** mean to you?

   _____

   _____

14) What is your fastest obstacle-course time? _____
15) When was the last time you played hide-and-seek? _____
16) Can you do high knee lifts? _____
17) If there were, say, a black-laced personal item lying on the laundry pile, would you:

    a. Say you have one just like it?
    b. Blush?
    c. Snicker?
18) If there were bags of dog food and water-softener salt pellets by the door, would you:
    a. Shove them over with your foot and keep on walking?
    b. Throw your coat on top of them?
    c. Use them to scrape the doggy-doo off the side of your shoe as you walk by?

FILL IN THE BLANK:
19) A woman's place _____
20) One thing I hope this application does not ask is

_____
_____

21) If I saw an apple core with a few ants on it, I would

_____
_____

22) Who is the beneficiary of your life insurance policy? _____
    Does it have an accidental injury clause? _____
23) Do you have a lawyer on retainer? _____
24) Are you available to serve as Sunbeam teacher? _____

I swear that all information supplied above is true and correct to the best of my knowledge under penalty of death, dismemberment, having fire-orange linoleum installed, electrocution, staple-gun puncturing, and hot-glue gun blistering.

Signature

_____

Thank you for your interest. Please allow four to six months for processing.
(And don't let the door hit you on your way out.)

Remember, folks, you're welcome anytime. My FRONT door is always open.

You Talked Me Into It

It's hard to slow the chaotic schedules and pace of life. There are so many options and choices out there to spend time on. I'm not really very good at slowing up. My husband has to help me out every once in a while, so every six months or so we have the same discussion.

"Guess what," I say.

He doesn't look up from his newspaper, but with a slight roll of his eyes, he says, "What?"

"A candidate for county commissioner called today and wondered if I would consider being his campaign manager!" No response from Fred. "A person doesn't get a call like that every day," I add.

Finally, "What'd you tell him?"

"I said I was overbooked until June, and by then the primaries would be over."

Fred looks back at his newspaper with—what was that, *relief?*

"That's good," he says. It looks like he wants to say more.

"What?!" I ask defensively.

Trying to look innocent, he says, "I didn't say anything."

"Don't you think that would have been . . . oh, I don't know. . . "

"Fun?" he finishes.

"Well, yeah, okay—fun. Is there something wrong with fun?"

And then comes the familiar part. "No, there's nothing wrong with fun, but . . ." He stops indecisively, like he's trying to decide if he's smart enough to keep his mouth shut or not.

"I know. You're going to say I never stick to anything."

"Do you?" The mouth-shut thing is apparently no longer an option.

"Yes. I stick to it as long as it's . . . well, it's . . ."

"Let me guess—fun?"

"That's not fair. I've stuck to a lot of things."

"Like the photography?"

"Oh, honey, that was years ago. Aren't you ever going to let me live that down? I just wanted to take a few pictures to go along with some newspaper articles."

"Was it $160 worth of fun? That was a lot of money for a camera in 1982. And then there was the $500 copier for some secretary thing."

"Well, okay, I had a rough beginning, but how about the candy-vending business—and the transcription? I've stuck to that for about five years now."

"And you've been trying to get out of both for four."

"Not the point."

"*Exactly* the point."

"Okay, maybe a *small* point."

I don't like the way Fred fights. In all fairness, I think he should let me justify everything I've tried. A few of them made money. Most of them at least brought a little excitement into our lives—*my* life. I like the thrill of the ups and downs, like a roller-coaster ride where you struggle and strain up one side, and then get that light-headed, losing-your-stomach rush swooping down the other. But the flat part, well that's just—flat.

He goes back to reading the newspaper, and I begin formulating my argument in my head. "How am I going to know what things are fun and what aren't, and what's challenging and what's not, what I'm good at and what I'm not unless I've tried them all? And ALL is a lot, so maybe I *should* get started on this one thing, so it won't get piled up when the next one arrives. You know how cranky I'll be if I get too much going on at once."

Scary, isn't it, when you can have an argument all by yourself?

Aloud I tell him simply, "You've talked me into it."

"What?" The newspaper is forgotten.

"I think I'll help with the campaign. Yep, it'll be the best thing for our marriage."

Marriage is a good thing. It's just sometimes hard and seems to *add* to the chaos of life. I especially hate that time of year when vacation schedules are passed around the office. I'm thinking there should be a law defining "vacation." My husband thinks a vacation is best spent puttering in his shop, or playing with his mules and wagon, or working on a backhoe—it doesn't matter what the project is with a backhoe, as long as he gets to run one. In the event that there is no current backhoe project to work on, he readily invents one. Which makes me think that this would be a grand idea for a men's theme park—a huge construction site where men get to pay their hundred bucks and run the construction equipment of their choice for the day, such as backhoes, earthmovers, Caterpillars. Basically anything that is really big, really greasy, and really noisy. The theme park should have a huge mountain in it with the idea that the men can move the mountain from one corner to another and back again. It's not like there has to be any actual sense to it—these are men after all. The park could also have a really big shop where men get to go "work on" their equipment, pretending that if they hammer loudly enough or heat something up with a cutting torch long enough, they can fix it. I'm telling you, this is a moneymaker. I'm a genius. But I digress . . .

My idea of a vacation is going out of town far enough to where the nearest washing machine, vacuum, and kitchen oven are a good eighty miles away, with wild animals within easy walking distance, and yet a convenient hamburger joint behind every other tree. It would also include museums and antique shops in abundance, and highway history markers—lots of highway history markers.

This year my husband gets three weeks of vacation instead of two. Now I ask you—is it wise to give two such people, who define "vacation" so differently, three weeks of vacation? Take it back, I say! It just means we have to have yet another discussion on what to do with it.

There are days when it's difficult to figure out why these piddly little irritations in life are oddly comforting—even the regular six-month "fun" conversation and the vacation-schedule discussion. I think it has something to do with Sunday evenings; there's a routine to it.

I love Sunday evenings. They're the best part of the week. The boys are usually in the living room watching another basketball game (or football game, or whatever season it is). Rachel is usually clipping snapshots for her scrapbook. Fred thumbs through the Sunday paper, and everyone crosses paths occasionally in the kitchen as they try to find something to eat. (Ha! Good luck, I say.) On a typical night, Rachel finally settles on a salad. Fred finds chips and salsa. Homer and Levi are still looking. The lawn is mowed and trimmed, the chickens are fed. I've had a lovely long nap, and Sunday is the only day I don't have to feel guilty for not doing laundry or cleaning the fridge or any one of a hundred things. And life is good. I glance at the TV, where half-time entertainment is in progress and the cameras scan the crowd, and I feel sorry for all those people who are not at home with their families, arguing over who's going to make popcorn and who took the last piece of cake, and wondering where the heck the remote is. I know many people would like to spend every spare moment out on a boat in the middle of a lake, or straddling ATVs on dirt trails, or something equally exciting, and still call it family time. But I maintain there is nothing quite like the time spent within the four walls of a home where there are no distractions and no diversions and only each other's personalities for excitement. That's where life happens. That's where we discuss vacation time and marriage issues and any one of a hundred other things. And it's comforting.

Then it's time for the weekly card game or dominoes game. Or maybe this week we'll play the Great Delmoody. Doesn't matter. Levi makes wisecracks, Will laughs at Levi's wisecracks, Homer tries everything (including cheating) to win, Rachel will probably do the actual winning, and Fred will refuse to play but will sit within a few feet of us at the computer or working on a puzzle so he can listen to it all. And Jenny will call on the telephone in a little while to see how our day went. And because it's so predictable I will soak it all in, be glad I'm part of it, and let it slow the pace for the upcoming week's chaos.

Beet Juice

It was funny at 9:30 in the morning. Beet juice. It's hilarious. Its purple-red spatters make the kitchen look like a crime scene, like some looney housewife went berserk and butchered the family rooster in the kitchen sink. The pickling syrup makes the kitchen smell like formaldehyde, and suddenly the beets take on a liver color and it feels like I'm in a morgue doing an autopsy. Okay, maybe that's not funny to you, but canning calls for desperate measures.

My fifteen-year-old daughter was "learning" home canning. She says she learns best with a loud radio on and obnoxious singing. *Singing* is her word, *obnoxious*—mine.

At 10:05 I yelled, "Rachel, turn down the radio!"

By 10:30 my toddling grandson was there enjoying the spatters as well. For his part, he threw a little Jell-o and a half-eaten ginger snap into the mess. He rearranged most of the cooking utensils on the floor for me to step over between sink and stove. (Who said grandmas aren't agile?) At 10:30 it was still funny even when I had to remind Rachel to turn down the radio.

By 12:00 two teenage boys that were there working on a shed were patiently waiting for dinner. Dinner? Did they expect me to feed them again? Breakfast was a mere five hours ago. Couldn't they come back tomorrow, when I could think? When I could hear myself?

"Rachel, TURN DOWN the radio!"

Would string cheese hold the boys over?

At 12:30 the washer repairman appeared—two days late. Nice of him to drop by. He was pleasant, quiet, and seemed to enjoy watching the spin cycle. For $196.83 I think I could be pleasant, quiet, and enjoy watching the spin cycle too. It's too bad he had to hear me scream, "Rachel, this is the last time. TURN DOWN THE RADIO."

By 1:30 the beet canner had boiled over with purple-brown juice so many times we quit wiping up the mess, and we had quit keeping track of which dishrag we wiped the floor with and which one we wiped dishes with (but we'll just keep that little secret to ourselves).

By 2:00 Rachel left the kitchen to dump beet skins over the fence while I hid her radio. (Shhh.)

By 3:00 the pickling spices weren't "autumn" smelling anymore, the vinegar mash smelled like old body odor, and no one was laughing. And did I mention my husband was home feeling under the weather for the second day in a row? As all wives know—that's never funny. Not in this lifetime.

By 4:28 there were four canner loads of beets left to process and not only was no one laughing, it was difficult to even be civil. My grandson went home, my daughter called a friend to commiserate, my son went to town, his friend left, and my husband hid in the bedroom.

At the end of the day I climbed into bed wondering why my mortal experience needed to have days like that in it. What, exactly, had we gained from it? Did I teach frugality? Did I impart the integrity of hard work? Did I gain patience? Did the kids learn that families work together? No . . . nothing so noble. I think a few jars of pickled beets is pretty much all we got. Some days are like that.

Some canning days are different. Sometimes I get a little meditation and quality contemplation in. Most of my inspiring ideas come while I'm standing at the kitchen sink, elbow-deep in dishwater or tomato skins. One fall in my steamy kitchen, not only did I slip tomato skins, scrub cukes, and make varicose veins scream, I also contemplated rising health-care costs. Clearly our lawmakers need help solving this issue, and I think they'd be a little surprised to find all the help they need embodied in kitchens across the country.

There was a day when a few jars of bread-and-butter pickles, a basket of beets, and a loaf of bread would buy the services of a doctor or midwife. A sack of potatoes, a peach pie, and a Rhode Island Red would fetch a heart specialist. It worked, too. People were grateful and generous. Nobody sued for malpractice. What would they have gained if they did? A crock of sauerkraut?

It's tempting to return to this system. Wouldn't you love to walk into the pediatrician's office today with a ham roast and two dozen eggs and ask for a tonsillectomy? It would probably make the doctor's gums bleed.

Of course, such astounding ideas only come to one who has stood at the sink all day waiting for the aspirin to kick in and hoping the steam from the pressure cooker doesn't make her freckles drip into the green-bean jars. Maybe more lawmakers should can garden produce. Maybe we all should. But ladies, I'm pooped. I can't solve all the national crises alone. So the next time you find yourself up to your elbows in pickling spices or beet juices, work on the national refuge problem, would you?

'Preciate that.

Chicken-Coop Compassion

Life's little clutters are a lot like chicken droppings—they need cleaning out once in a while.

I have laying hens, did I tell you that? I enjoy hens. They aren't needy like dogs and cats, always begging for affection and attention. I can basically ignore a chicken. Never pet it, never talk to it, never take it to the veterinarian, never bathe it, never buy little treats or toys for it. And yet each and every morning it gives me something productive—something useful. That's my kind of pet.

Nonetheless, in exchange for those eggs I do have to deal with chicken droppings. Did you know that the best way to clean chicken doo-doo out of the coop is to soak it first? It shovels better wet. (Well, actually the *very best* way to clean the coop is to hire a deacon who wants to earn money for Scout camp.) The hens do seem appreciative when they have a clean coop. I'm not sure how I know this, actually, as it's difficult to read a chicken. They really don't purr or wag their feathers.

People aren't so different. We have to clean the doo-doo out of our lives periodically, as well. This is what goal setting and New Year's resolutions are all about—cleanup. About cleaning the doo-doo out of our lives. Getting rid of the clutter.

This is my clutter-cleaning shortlist of resolutions:

THE GOOD NEWS: I am not beaten! I *will* read another classic novel. Just because I can't sit through opera, ballet, or symphonies, and can't paint or sing, I will *not* give up on culturing myself. There's got to be some refinement in me, just waiting for a chance to be discovered.

THE BAD NEWS: My library card expired. Neither can I buy a book, because the overwhelming latte smell in the bookstore makes me nauseated. Those classics have lasted this long without me; they'll just have to last a little longer.

THE GOOD NEWS: I have no intention of losing ten pounds. I'm a grandma now. The only thing anyone expects me to lose is my memory.

THE BAD NEWS: I will still pathetically *consider* losing another ten pounds . . . I will still definitely *plan* on considering losing ten pounds—and who am I kidding? It should be fifteen.

THE GOOD NEWS: I read a home fix-it book that explained that I—yes, even I—can replace the cracked tile around the tub and regrout it.

THE BAD NEWS: It did not explain how to pay for this little project, or how to pay for the professional I will have to call in to bail me out of the screwups this causes, or how to tell the occupants of my home that they cannot use the shower for three weeks while I figure these things out.

THE GOOD NEWS: I plan on being kinder this year.

THE BAD NEWS: It's going to be extremely hard to be kind if I get even *one more telemarketing phone call!*

The problem with these resolutions (okay, *one* of the problems) is that I defeat myself before I even start. But besides that, knowing exactly what to clean out is difficult, too. In a chicken coop it's not difficult. I get the biggest snow-shovel scoop I can find and start in one corner, pushing out everything that will move and doesn't hop over the shovel. In life, however, there are things that shouldn't be scooped out. Choosing "the good part" is the key. Like Sister Bonnie D. Parkin said, "Wouldn't it be easy if we were choosing between visiting teaching or robbing a bank? Instead, our choices are often more subtle. We must choose between many worthy options" (*Ensign,* Nov. 2003, 104). Picking and choosing becomes a problem when I attack it with a scoop. This year I'm going to throw out my shortlist scoop and new resolutions. This year I will focus on not scooping out charity along with the poop. I will have more compassion for mankind, namely:

I will have compassion for birthday-party moms who inherit leftover hot dogs, extra socks, swimming towels, and the blame for not having enough sunscreen.

I will have compassion for Little League coaches who inherit parental wrath and sunglasses tans.

I will have compassion for grandmas who swim with grandkids regardless of their cellulite. They sow memories for children.

I will have compassion for the basketball-grandstand moms, aunts, and uncles who inherit backaches, swollen ankles, and half-eaten suckers.

I will have compassion for park groundskeepers who inherit overflowing trash cans and picnic tables dotted with chewing gum.

I will have compassion for baseball-tournament schedulers, for the wind is bound to blow and the rains, determined to descend, heedless of games, only to cease ten minutes after the last batter has swung.

I will have compassion for four-year-old children who come to park concession stands with big, beaming smiles and a sense of wonder at finding a bright, shiny penny in the grass, wanting to know what it can buy.

I will have compassion for children who come to the concession stand counters with fifty cents clutched tightly in their hands, surrounded by at least three friends all begging to have a piece of whatever they buy.

I will have compassion for grandpas who come to the park walking dogs, or to find a bench under the trees where they can escape the heat of the day and take a nice nap while the kids on the merry-go-round flip sand in their faces.

I will have compassion for kids who have jobs and show up at 6:30 A.M. to mow grass, pick up trash, and wash down park bathrooms.

I will have compassion for grandparents who bring kids to swimming lessons, pack quarters for treats afterwards, and haul wet kids back home again in their nice, very clean cars.

And I will have more compassion for me. I won't be hard on myself for not getting dinner done on time, for letting weeds overtake the garden, for letting the dust collect. Because we're all just folks— just plain, regular folks living our lives the best we know how.

And that's my new set of resolutions. The good news is it really cuts through the poop. It's very productive and useful. The bad news is that even if I accomplish these goals, like the chickens, I will still basically be ignored. Never petted, never sweet-talked, never taken to the veterinarian, never bathed, never have little treats or toys bought for me. And yet each and every morning I will be expected to produce breakfast.

Back to School

There's nothing like taking a college class to make you feel really stupid. I chose a mining class for my torture this summer. How hard could it be? I figured I'd be listening to folklore about miners who lost their mules and chased their dogs down gopher holes until they struck veins of gold. I thought we'd be visiting mining ghost towns and experimenting with panning for gold. Instead, I found out what a chemistry lesson was like without Ken and Charlie.

Ken and Charlie were the ones who got me through high school chemistry. Ken and Charlie understood $2PbS + 4FeO.SiO + 2C = 2Pb2FeS + FeO.SiO2 + 2CO$. I just nodded occasionally to encourage them. Where were Ken and Charlie when I needed them this summer?

Geologic terms are Greek to me. Actually, most of the terms *are* Greek. Sphalerite for zinc—in Greek, that means "treacherous." (If Americans ran around buck-naked posing for athletic contests and not having to worry about little things like CLOTHES, we could come up with great Greek words too, I think.)

Our mining instructor worked for the Environmental Protection Agency, and while I was trying to pull the periodic table from the cobwebbed tombs of memory, he rattled off formulas like we all knew what he was talking about. I just nodded from time to time, and this seemed to encourage him. Amazing how a little nod makes a man think you're actually listening. He kept using the words "stope," "winze," "salting," "jigging," "float," "cribbing," and "adit." I tried to make up an austere, philosophic Greek definition for each word, but I suppose it's harder when one is not athletically posed à la fresco.

He also pointed out several things that I hadn't known. Things like why you can't drive from southern Idaho to northern Idaho without going through Montana, Oregon, or Washington—it's because of the Idaho batholith. Cool word, that—batholith. It kinda gets caught in cotton on your tongue. I also learned that Idaho's panhandle boundaries were drawn up largely because of politically volatile mining problems in Coeur d'Alene—Washington and Montana just cut it out, and what was left was a panhandle that no one wanted.

I learned how to tell if bats were using an old mine shaft, but the rest of the two-day lecture went right over my head. A waste of perfectly good brain cells.

But there was one important part—I got to buy a Lunchable (those prefab lunches I always bought for kids' field trips). The food is arranged in such cute little compartments. I'd wanted one of those forever, but couldn't ever justify the lousy three bucks.

But I'm a grandma now. I'm due. For *my* field trip I bought a Lunchable! It's a good thing Ken and Charlie weren't there after all. It was a pretty small serving and I would have hated to share. And even *with* their help, I only got a B in Chemistry. Camaraderie only goes just so far.

Callings: How I Learned to Say No—Not!

President Hinckley said: "I invite every one of you, wherever you may be as members of this church, to stand on your feet and with a song in your heart move forward, living the gospel, loving the Lord, and building the kingdom. Together we shall stay the course and keep the faith, the Almighty being our strength" (*Ensign*, Nov. 1995, 72). I'm certainly trying to keep this counsel, but it's not very easy.

One Sunday, not long ago, I had come home from church with a wet dress after a particularly trying day in the nursery. One little girl came into the nursery, and as she did every week, she curled up on my lap for a good hour or so before she would crawl down to play with the other kids. But this particular Sunday as she sat curled in my lap, I felt something wet. I checked—the diaper had leaked. We found the child's mother and she changed the little girl and brought her back, where she again crawled up onto my lap, but with a wet dress. I couldn't resist her. She needed a lap to curl in. So I cradled her and decided our dresses would just have to dry later. Basically, if we throw in a few runny noses and soggy shortbread cookies, that pretty well summarizes the whole nursery calling.

Whatever made them call me to the nursery again? I already know the answer—no one else will say yes, and I can't say no. Suffice it to say, I have already done several nursery stints. Didn't that bishop's counselor realize how many eensy-weensy spiders I have washed away and how the popcorn has popped on the apricot tree so many times it really isn't such a nice surprise anymore? I have hokey-pokey-ed and ring-around-the-rosy-ed. I have shipped Moses down the river wrapped in doll blankets in a basket cradle. I have picked dandelions and made paper chains, put together broken puzzles and read the same Curious George book several hundred times. And every week there are diaper *issues*.

Serving in the nursery was one of the very first callings I ever had. I wasn't excited, but I couldn't say no. I'm not sure I gained any points in heaven for just "not being able to say no," but I endured.

A few years after that first nursery calling, my wonderful bishop came to the house, sat on the couch and squirmed a bit, then said, "Sister Jaynes, we need a new Relief Society president. So I prayed and studied it out and your name came to mind . . . so I went back and prayed some more."

I swear I'm not making this up. I was stunned that he would admit this.

"A couple weeks went by. After I prayed again, your name came to mind . . . again." Long pause. Way too long of a pause.

"I decided to pray harder."

I looked across the room at my husband. Was he kidding? I looked back at that sweet man who was clearly squirming now, and thought, "If you think this is difficult for *you*, buddy, think again!"

He continued, "A few more weeks went by and I took the matter to the Lord again. Guess whose name I thought of?"

Hmmm.

"So, Sister Jaynes, THE LORD is calling you to be the next Relief Society president."

I was speechless.

Instead of just not being able to say no, I mustered all my faith together and accepted the call. Then I endured washing dishes through all the ward parties, listening to all the reasons sisters gave to not go visiting teaching, and walking into the bishop's office where the brethren had already been meeting for an hour in close quarters, and the air was thick with cologne from early-morning meetings. Of course that wasn't the calling; that was just details.

I still had a scrap of faith left years later when a stake priesthood leader called me and said, "Sister Jaynes, we're trying to find a cook for stake girls' camp. Can you go?"

"But President, I don't even *like* to cook."

"Just throw a few hot dogs in a pan. It'll be great."

"This is *girls'* camp. Not Scout camp. That won't cut it for girls."

"You've cooked for a family. How bad can you be?"

"You'd be surprised."

"Well, we've already asked literally fifteen or sixteen people who all said no. Would you do it?" It was so comforting to know I was *seventeenth* on the list. I felt so wanted. I am still stunned that fifteen or sixteen people absolutely *could* say no. Was I the only one with this problem? Of course I went.

I fried bacon at five o'clock in the morning, panicked through the oh-no, I-forgot-to-order-hamburger-buns moment, and was too tired to attend evening firesides.

Then one night I got a call from that same stake priesthood leader who had asked me to cook at girls' camp, and he said, "Sister Jaynes, we need a speaker at a stake youth fireside in two days. Can you do it?" Because I was teaching seminary, working full time, still had six adults living in my home, and was a little stressed, I asked (and I should have known better), "Why such short notice?"

He said (and *he* really should have known better), "We tried everyone else . . ."

What *was* it with me and callings? How could I *be* so lucky?

"President, I was the last choice? The *last* choice? Just *once* I'd like to be the first choice. Why don't you ever call me *first?*"

Perhaps I've come full circle. I went from not being able to say no, to making a pretty good stab at faithfulness, to patient endurance. There's a pretty fine line between them, I think. So subtle, in fact, that perhaps in some ways they're the same thing.

"I invite every one of you, wherever you may be as members of this church, to stand on your feet and with a song in your heart move forward, living the gospel, loving the Lord, and building the kingdom. Together we shall stay the course and keep the faith, the Almighty being our strength" (*Ensign*, Nov. 1995, 72).

In nursery I'm certainly not always standing on my feet, the song in my heart sometimes repeats "Eensy Weensy Spider" like a broken record, and it feels like I'm working in circles more than moving forward, but like the rest of the women I know in the Church, we are certainly trying to live the gospel, love the Lord, build the kingdom, stay the course, and keep the faith. Thank goodness the Almighty has the strength for it.

The Baddest: My Conscience Returns

On a scale of one to ten with one being the "baddest," if I buy someone a birthday present and then keep it for myself instead—how bad is that? Hypothetically, if we call that a "five," then how bad would it be if I bought the person *another* present, but ended up keeping that one as well? Three maybe? Then just where on the scale would it fit if I bought a *fourth* birthday present, kept it on the shelf out of sight for two whole months to give as a birthday gift (yes, all for the same birthday), but finally took it down and kept that too?

I knew it—I'm going to you-know-where. And that is why it is now March and my sister has not received her January birthday gift. That is also why I have the cutest little pig-on-a-swing hanging in my dining room window—I originally bought it for my mom on Mother's Day. It's why I have a darling little chicken sitting on my desk at work that was intended for my daughter. I'm bad. I'm bad. I'm bad.

I wonder if I've *always* been this bad?

Well, actually, there was the time when as a child I took a candy bar from the cupboard without asking my mom. Then the next day I felt so guilty, I asked her if I *could* have one, and then didn't take it just to make things even again.

If only my conscience would give me a break now and then. If I didn't have to constantly scrutinize and analyze, I might have so much brain capacity freed that I could . . . I could . . . well, see—I can't even come up with anything, that's how totally consumed I am. My conscience is wired so tight that I can barely survive a background check.

I know because one of my employers recently required a back-ground check before hiring me. It began with a polygraph test of sorts. They clipped on a microphone and asked me questions, and the computer determined stress levels by the little radio waves emitted. The theory is that if a person is stressed when answering a question, then she's being deceptive. The result was that, according to the machine, I spent one and a half hours lying. I flunked the first two tests! Incredible. My greatest fear going into the test was that I would find a way to screw it up. Evidently, I did. These are the questions I kept flunking: (1) Have you used marijuana? (2) Have you used cocaine? (3) Have you had sexual relations in the workplace? and (4) Have you stolen more than $300 from an employer? Finally, the test administrator said "I'll ask these ONE MORE TIME." I don't know whether I passed or he just gave up.

I found out that not only am I consciously bad, but I also have failings that I was completely oblivious to. The same employer also required a hearing test. I assumed that was important because I would have headphones on, trying to transcribe—yes, that makes sense. After the hearing test the lady told me, "Ma'am, you have a hearing loss." I explained that I was forty-five years old (flattering myself that she couldn't already tell), and that after forty a little bit of everything went. I certainly already knew I couldn't hear the phone ring from outside, or the oven timer from the other end of the house, but really—who my age can? She said, "No, ma'am, you have a hearing loss. It's in the range that blocks out vowel sounds and consonant." No vowels and consonants? A statement like that simply begs the question, "WHAT ELSE IS THERE, HONEY????"

Then I went to an occupational therapist who was supposed to run a battery of tests to see whether I could move. I thought it might be obvious if I showed up for the job interview that I could *move.* There was only one surprise there—the therapist spent quite a bit of time trying to determine whether I had carpal tunnel signs or not (important if you're a cocaine-sniffing, marijuana-smoking, sexy klep-tomaniac who is using her wrists to type, I suppose). The good news was that there were no carpal tunnel signs. The bad news was that the strengths of the two major muscles in my forearm, the little ulnar muscle (which is supposed to be weak) and the flexor radialis (which is supposed to be strong), were reversed. No one told me when I was growing up to pay attention to which muscle did what. Maybe it came from years of cow milking. I asked who really cared, but the therapist seemed to think I ought to work on it. Yeah, right. I'll just fit that in somewhere between ALL MY OTHER exercises—you know, like buying marijuana.

Well, later the employer called me back and offered me a job. Is that not just the goofiest thing you've ever heard of? I should have skipped the whole résumé and interview business and just written:

To Whom It May Concern:

I think you should hire me because I'm old and hard of hearing—but don't worry, I only miss vowels and consonants. When I type I'll probably wear out the keys that my little finger pounds too hard, and I once stole $300 from an employer, and bought cocaine and marijuana with it. Then I had an inappropriate relationship in the workplace, sniffed the cocaine and smoked the marijuana, and FORGOT THE WHOLE THING. When can I start?

P.S. Please don't expect me to bring birthday gifts to other office workers. My conscience just can't handle it.

This is going to sound silly, but I really thought at one point that a person as flawed as I was could find no niche in this world, let alone the sisterhood of Relief Society. It's so easy to think of myself as the only woman with holes in her character—or the only woman with holes in her character but a cute pig-on-a-swing. I perceive that if the other Relief Society sisters were cheeses, they would be cheddar, American, and Roquefort. I, on the other hand, would be Swiss—full of holes, holes, holes. Comfortingly enough, there is even a niche for Swiss in this fledgling kingdom of God.

The Other Journal

I woke up at four o'clock this morning and lay in the dark, as I so often do these days, examining my life. Only this time I woke up with a stress headache. Those are different from normal headaches. In order to shake these off I need deep sleep and caffeine—which automatically cancel each other out, so they're difficult to deal with. I tried to figure out which part of my life was stressful enough to bring this headache on, and I didn't have to think long. My job brought it on, and again I had to wonder exactly why it was that I began working.

For years I had patched together odd jobs and home businesses so that I could stay at home with the kids, and I felt so smart for doing so. Twenty-five years later the debts had mounted considerably. There were surgeries for broken bones, torn ligaments to reattach, tire replacements for cars, alternators that went out, insurance premiums that raised (even though income didn't), career changes for my husband, and a farm, many years ago, that had left us with lifetime debt. So I faced the inevitable. I would get a job.

This was difficult to do. I was middle-aged and had no résumé to speak of. I had driven a sugar-beet and spud trucks during harvests. I cleaned a restaurant once after it had been repossessed. I serviced a candy-vending route. I taught classes at the local community college off and on. But future employers didn't care. I hadn't learned "job skills." In the eyes of most employers, I wasn't exactly hireable material.

What I HAD learned over the years got me into considerable trouble. I had learned I was as competent as the next person; that even if the other guy had a college degree or titles, it didn't make his

I.Q. any higher and his life experiences didn't make him any more capable or any better a human being—only richer. I learned that no matter how important someone thought he was, his bluff wouldn't work on me. I also learned that it was my style to be in charge. I was doomed.

The first problem was that, if nothing else, all the collected debt had taught me to do math. Hence, I already knew I couldn't work cheaply or for minimum wage—I'd be losing money. So I was looking for a higher-paying, unskilled job.

After months of looking, I was hired to run an office (I thought). This I could do, and that was the problem. The employer really didn't want me to run it any differently than it was already being run. And she didn't want me to know more about any aspect of its management than she did, as in computer programs, etc.—that was a threat to her control. My problem was that I was too old to be told when to move and how to move when I could think for myself, thank you. We were both unhappy. I lasted six weeks before I began job hunting again.

The next job was working for another control freak. (I can pick 'em, can't I?) About two months later my employer and I had a "discussion." At the end of the discussion, his face was red, his neck veins were bulging, and he was literally yelling. I was calm, collected, and best of all—right. That's what got me fired the following week. It's just as well. What he really needed was a younger person who would tell him periodically that he was amazing and wonderful. It just wasn't in me.

On the day I was fired that time, I was rehired by five o'clock. Other employers in the same office obviously saw things differently than the first boss did. They did, however, adjust my hours, which is still a concern to me. So, each and every day I still wonder what in the heck I'm doing at a job.

In the meantime, I haven't baked Christmas goodies this year, because there has been no time or I've been too tired. I didn't get any canning done this fall for the same reasons. I have a simple little cold that is roaring into its fourth week now. I have a quilt top ready to piece together, grandchildren needing to be spoiled, and that cobweb in the corner of the house has *got* to come down eventually. But I just can't get to it. I have one child left in high school and I'm not here when she comes home, and it's killing me. I miss hearing about her day at school. And haven't we been counseled by our prophets not to work outside the home? That guilt gets heavier each day, too. On the other hand, there is our insurmountable debt and the counsel to get out of debt. So I have no peace.

I wonder how other women do it. Sometimes I wish working women could sit in church and have an open and candid discussion about it. Talking about debt is tricky, though, because counsel from our leaders has been not to have it! So to discuss it openly would be to admit that we have not been obedient in that regard. Talking about women working is tricky too, without judging each other. Everyone comes away offended, whether it was intentional or not. It would make for a more lively Relief Society, though. I'm pretty sure everyone on the widows' row would stay awake.

I'm not sure very many sisters that work are really happy, yet some have obviously come to have peace. How I wish for their counsel!

Here I sit, middle-aged, too old to be diplomatic, unaccustomed to office-personnel maneuvers, unwilling to work for minimum wage, with a lousy résumé and a headache that won't quit. And I *went looking* for this! I deserve every bit of this nasty headache. I'm not so smart after all. That's why I must write about this. But it won't go into my regular journal. It will have to go into my *other* journal.

The *other* journal began a few years ago when I was experiencing some rather heavy trials in my personal life. Relationships were strained beyond what I felt like I could handle. I contemplated major changes. I was alternately angry and strong, or overwhelmed and completely powerless. Different people handle their trials differently when frustrated. When I was younger I used to play the piano when I was angry, or sad, or happy. Some find it therapeutic to work out at the gym, or sew, or garden, or even kick the dog. These days, when I can't handle life any longer, I turn to my journal and write. I found, however, that I was writing some pretty nasty stuff in my journal and, after all, I think a journal should be instructive and encouraging— something one hands down to one's children.

That's when I began the *other* journal. The first journal will be the one I hand down to the kids, and I will be truthful but discreet in what I write there. The *other* journal is for the nastiness. It's the one where I whine and complain—where I'm negative, belittling, sarcastic, judgmental, and critical. I write about my weaknesses, the times I haven't been as valiant as I should have been. In the *other* journal I also write about the hurts I have received at the hands of others—plenty of hurts. I write about the humiliation, the sorrow, the anger, and the pity I have felt for myself. It is the ugly journal, the journal I'm not proud of, the journal no one can ever read, the one I will have to burn before I die.

About the same time as I began the *other* journal, something else was happening as well. I had just read a conference issue of the *Ensign* and what caught my eye and my heart was the fact that whenever the General Authorities talked about Jesus Christ or the Atonement, there was a depth there that I somehow couldn't lock into. They *knew* something that I didn't. I wanted to *know* what it was they knew— not in an arrogant way so that I could be as great as they are, but only so that my heart could reach the depth of what they knew about the Atonement. I could feel that depth was there somewhere; I just couldn't grasp it—couldn't process it in my head.

I began a focused search. I read the New Testament accounts of the Crucifixion, and because there is such a paucity of detail there, I really didn't learn anything new. I read certain conference talks over again looking for some clue. I read talks about repentance, because I knew it was sin that Christ had atoned for. I prayed for more under- standing. I read some of the more familiar discourses like King Benjamin's address and Alma the Younger's counsel to his sons. I was certainly enriched, but I didn't feel any closer to understanding the Atonement. Something wasn't clicking.

I'm so grateful to my Heavenly Father for the timing of these two events—searching for the depths of Atonement and creating the *other* journal. One day I was contemplating the Atonement again, going over everything I'd read, searching for some clue that I'd missed, when unexpectedly the thought popped into my head (and simultaneously sank into my heart) "the *other* journal—the Atonement is not just for sin, it's also for the *other* journal." And suddenly the Atonement came into very clear focus. All of what the scriptures had been trying to say and all that the general conference talks had expressed now felt within my understanding. The Atonement could help me through all the nastiness, all the sarcasm and sorrow, all the pain inflicted by the choices of myself and others.

Now, here I lay at four o'clock in the morning with a stress headache, in a mid-life job crisis, with employers who are sometimes small and demeaning, with my own impatience, with the burden of past debt hanging over me, with my heart breaking with the desire to be home again, and I know that I will once again turn to the *other* journal, and to the Atonement to see me through. That is my peace.

SEASON IV

The Simmering Pot

When I Am Old

I used to have some goals that I thought were "lofty" and would challenge me. Among them, I wanted to finish the bachelor's degree that I neglected in order to raise a family, I wanted to be "significantly" recognized for writing, and I wanted to speak at a major women's conference. I don't know what I thought these particular goals would do for me, but when I was younger and wanted to "escape" the drudgery of whatever I was doing, I daydreamed about these goals and how I would accomplish them, and (not so humbly) how accomplished I would feel when I achieved them. I guess I rather immodestly thought they would somehow make me noble or important. But, truthfully, they're not my highest priority anymore. Time has had a way of modifying them.

My new list is quite long and is now much more humble, to wit:

I hope I will remember that there are plenty of young mothers out there whose children need just a little bit of spending money and, more importantly, an opportunity to learn to work. When my own children are grown, I will hire a youth to mow my lawn, even if I can do it myself. Even if my house is immaculate and my garden never grows a weed (hey—it could happen) I will hire a child to help me. I will hire one to pick asparagus and strawberries and chokecherries. I will make it a point to hit a few yard sales with lemonade stands and buy a cup or two. Even if my car was washed yesterday, I will support the local youth car wash—and not just donate. I will make them wash the car!

I will take grandchildren shopping to Deseret Industries, give them a couple dollars and see if they can find a really great buy, or take them to the dollar store before Mother's Day and Father's Day for shopping. I will find a child to help with a paper route some morning. I will help with a science project.

I will hand-make gifts for young family members for their hope chests.

I will organize a holiday family reunion, and have already started that endeavor:

Dear Offspring (some springy-er than others),

The annual get-together will be on (date) , for those interested in attending. Anyone who RSVPs by (date) will have sleeping arrangements made for them. Here's our plan:

Friday night:

6–9:00 PM: Soup and homemade bread served, with sundaes served at 9:00 P.M. Dish detail: ages 5–15, (adult) supervising. Evening of videos and visiting and scrapbooking.

Saturday:

8–9:00 AM: Grandpa's special pancake-and-waffle breakfast. Dish detail: ages 16–25, (adult) supervising.

10–12:00 PM: Snow games and wagon rides with Grandpa Fred's mules, cutting firewood, and quilting with Grandma Lynn.

12–1:00 PM: Lunch—light sandwiches (looking for a volunteer to organize and prepare). Ages 26–35 on dish detail, (adult) supervising.

2:00 PM: Family picture, casual attire.

4–5:00 PM: Traditional family holiday dinner. Dish detail: ages 36–45, (adult) supervising.

6–9:00 PM: Gift exchange. (All gifts provided by Grandpa and Grandma!) Short video of holidays past. Card games and board games. Treats!

9:00 PM: Family prayer and children to bed.

9:00 PM–?:   Parents' time with chips, dip, and desserts. Cleanup detail: anyone still awake.

Sunday:

8–9:00 AM: Repeat of Grandpa's breakfast. Dish detail: men, (female) supervising.

11:30 AM: Church. Lunch after church—potato bar with salad. Dish detail: women, (female) supervising. Supper is everyone for himself—whatever he can forage. (Stay as late as you want, but Grandpa and Grandma have to be to bed by 10:00 P.M.)

(Or maybe we'll throw in a little line dancing, Dutch-oven cooking, or visit graves even though it's not Memorial Day.)

Love you all!
Mom

I will pick up some little family members from their homes early in the morning when they're still in their pajamas, and take them to breakfast at a restaurant for a pajama party.

I will hold Thanksgiving on Friday so that families are not torn between relatives and making their own traditions. I will make gingerbread houses. I will pull taffy. I will hold an Old Woman's Academy and invite young children to attend for the day, teaching them any skill they don't usually have exposure to—perhaps puppeteering, fonduing, pressing flowers, or visiting local museums.

I will send phone "coupon books" to the nieces, nephews, and grandkids (i.e. "This coupon is good for one call to say good night," "This coupon is good for one call to sing me a new Primary song,"

"This coupon is good for one call to practice your Primary talk," "This coupon is good for one call to tell me how the track meet went," etc.).

I will help a child start a collection, and I shall keep a jar of coins handy to buy into their latest fund-raising project. I will send a child little tricks or jokes to perform as part of family home evening. I will write down spiritual stories about myself from different times in my life and send them to a child.

I will make a story jar and fill it with paraphernalia and mementos from spiritual stories; each time a child asks me to tell a story about my youth, I can let them pull out an item from my jar and I will relate the accompanying story.

When I am old, I hope I will remember to wear vanilla-bean perfume so that grandchildren will snuggle near me on the church bench. I hope I'll remember to carry a roll of Lifesavers in my purse and a hankie that I can fold into a cradle with babies—that'll occupy the restless child who crawls under the pews. When I am old (yet not so very old) I hope I will keep a box of fabric scraps for little girls to fashion doll clothes from, and teach them to cut quilt blocks, because mothers don't have much time for that.

When my hair is gray and my feet are slow, I want to remember to invite a child to go fishing with me to bait my hooks. Or maybe I'll invite some little girls over for a tea party with open-faced sandwiches and cream puffs and pink punch. I hope I remember how to visit about dollies, dandelions, milkweed worms, and such. I hope I remember to put a dish of mint candies on the table and doilies on the armchair. And dresses . . . I want to wear lots of dresses.

When my eyes are dim and I'm using those ugly magnifying spectacles, I hope I remember to sit in a swing and feel the breeze lift my gray hairs. I hope I remember how to flip my shoes up onto the roof from the swing set. I hope when businesses retire me and life seems quiet, that I will remember children need old women to wave back at them as they look through the back window of the school bus. I hope I remember that children don't care what old women look like at the swimming pool, and that kids don't care if grandmas have purple spider veins in their legs or "Relief Society" arms that waddle in the breeze—in fact, they find it rather fascinating. I hope I won't worry about my hair getting wet, but will just have fun splashing with them. And inner tubes . . . I will rent an inner tube at the swimming pool.

When my hearing is fading and I can't understand the church sermon, the theater, the plays, or school programs, I hope I remember to go anyway; I can still clap. Performers need lots of clappers. Or I can bow my head for the prayer.

I will let the kids eat all the chocolate bars that were meant for s'mores before we get to the mountains—or half of them anyway. I hope I think to take them to the hills to pick chokecherries. I've got to remind myself to show them the museum in the old schoolhouse. I must remember that kids like to draw rings on their fingers with ink pens and wear watermelon-red fingernail polish. They need lots of bubble gum and jokes . . . kids like jokes.

I must show my grandchildren, nieces, and nephews how to find Scorpio and Orion, and how to press wildflowers in a book. I must ask them to help me feed the birds and squirrels, and I'll show them how to take their newly cut hair and let it drift in the wind for birds to use in building their nests.

When I am old, I want to have cubbyholes in my house for children to discover—little nooks and crannies where they can hide from their mother, especially when she's late and in a real hurry. I want to have a sturdy poplar tree for them to climb when their grandpa finds his broken hammer and is looking for "those little monsters."

I will teach them how to race Daddy's tape measures on his workbench. I will teach them how to skate over the carpet in their socks, building up static so that when Grandpa falls asleep in the chair they can shock his whiskers. I will stitch a pillow for my backside so that I can sit on the floor and teach them to play jacks. I will teach them how to carefully peek in their Christmas gifts. I will sneak them olives and bites of turkey at Thanksgiving—before dinner. I will teach them how to eat the chocolates from the nut cups and slip the peanuts into their daddy's cup. I have so much to teach them.

I will have to remember what embarrasses them, too—things like clicking dentures, complaining of aches and pains, driving with the left blinker on since 1997, or driving with the seat belt hanging out the car door for a three-mile stretch, or discussing doctor visits and smelling like moth balls.

I must remember to fix wheat mush every morning or hot milk, and toast with melted butter, because, of course, children will expect strange foods of me. Even though they won't like it, I think it will make them feel comfortable. I will remember to sit with a little "humph."

I seriously doubt that I will ever have the means again to finish my bachelor's degree, that being "significantly" recognized for writing is going to make me any happier, and I already spoke at a major women's conference—which didn't make me "important" at all. I think these new goals will be much more meaningful. I do, however, have much to get done in the next few years. I think I have the ring-drawing on the fingers almost perfected, and I like wheat mush already. But where is Orion, anyway?

A Bite of Cake

When we moved Mom into our home three years ago, none of us really knew what we were in for, and we don't know what's around the next three-year corner either, except change, I suppose. Hard change. Always change. As I watched Mom go through this ordeal at seventy, I realized that even though I'm all grown up now, I still have much to go through. So much to learn—how to grow old, how to move homes again, how to be useful to my family when they're old enough to take care of themselves, and how to make that wonderful chocolate cake.

On that day, Mom stood at her stove stirring a pot while we (her children, our spouses, and kids) carried her belongings out the door. I watched the first boxes as they went by, every box labeled with mother's small handwriting—bandages, hot-water bottles, embroidery hoops. She was great at organizing. But then I noticed something.

"Mom, I thought you said you packed things up. There are only eight boxes here."

Mom looked up from her wire whisk. "Well, I did. That's as far as I got." She went back to stirring.

Mom had become nervous about living on her own. She was afraid she might fall, and her eyesight was beginning to fail. After all of her ten children had proffered invitations to live with them, she finally accepted ours. Our family was nearly grown, and we were still close to her doctors and hometown. We converted a small living room into a bedroom for her and this was moving day.

From the back bedroom someone yelled, "Granny, come in here. We don't know what you want packed up and what you don't."

Mom swirled little figure eights in the steam rising from her pot and seemed not to notice. Finally, I stood from sorting cupboard contents and went to the bedroom. My husband Fred held up a glass bowl.

"No, don't take that," I said. "My house isn't big enough for any more fluted dishes."

"What do we do with it?"

"I'm not sure. Set it in a pile on the living room floor, I guess."

Fred and our son Levi carried out the mattress, then the box springs, the headboards, and finally the nightstands and packed them tightly into a horse trailer. The heirloom beveled mirror, hollow ostrich egg, and kerosene lamps were wrapped separately in quilts, carried out one by one, and placed in the pickup cab. Trip after trip the boys panted and groaned, passing Mom. She didn't look up.

They were carrying off fifty years of her life. Still Mom stirred the pot. Her egg bucket on the shelf nearby held golden-colored eggs with little bits of straw still clinging to them. Her cotton gloves were stuck over the hoe and rake handles in the corner. The garden hat and black-rubber irrigating boots waited behind the door. Fred picked them up and tossed them to Levi, who threw them all in the pile on the living room floor.

Among the usual sounds of moving, phrases like, "Can we have the vacuum? . . . That is, if you don't need it," or, "I could really use those spices in my food storage," or "I've always wanted a roaster pan" were heard.

After a while no one bothered asking anymore. Things just moved out, disappeared—boxes of gaudy outdated jewelry, Christmas bulbs and lights, pale-green drinking glasses, doilies and ironed pillow slips, umbrellas, a manual typewriter, and hummingbird feeders.

I walked to the stove again. "Mom, they really need you in the bedroom. You have to tell them what to take." The pot was bubbling now. "Are you feeling all right?" I paused, for the first time looking into the pot. Mom didn't respond.

"Mom, why are you cooking today, of all days?"

She lifted the pot from the stove and poured chocolate frosting onto a cake.

"I just thought you kids might like a bite of cake. I know you like chocolate." She smoothed the top of the cake with the butter knife and padded to the sink to set the frosting pan to soak. Her thin shoulder blades stuck out sharply. It took both of her arthritic hands working together to turn the faucet off. I brushed her cold hands as I reached over to swipe some frosting.

"Sounds great, Mom, but we need your help. We don't know what to take. We don't know what's important to you."

"You decide." She swept the butter knife back and forth across the cake top. "All I need is my clothes and my bed." She carried the cake to the table with a lopsided gait and set some chipped, pink-flowered dishes beside it, then sat down.

I went to the back bedroom again and swept up the balls of lint and dust that had collected under the dresser and bed. The boys were in the front room maneuvering a chair through the doorframe. I sat down against the wall of the back bedroom. If I tried, I could almost picture where my own bed and dresser had stood forty years ago. I'd had a pink nubby bedspread then and a hand-me-down doll cradle. I don't remember my doll's name now.

The sound of Fred's footsteps in the hallway startled me. His steps sounded just like my father's used to. I got up and went back to the kitchen.

"Mom, this must be hard for you," I said. Mom didn't answer. She watched the boys fumble with TV cords and tools. I looked at her hands, then at the clock, and back at her hands again. Probably that was the wrong thing to say. What was the *right* thing?

"Mom, would you like me to ask everyone to leave now and go through things privately with you?"

"No, no," Mom insisted, "it doesn't matter."

I tried again. "You'll want to decorate your new room. What do you want to hang on the walls?"

Mom gazed slowly around her paneled walls at the gold roses framed on black velvet, the oil-on-canvas landscape nearby signed *To Mom, Love Christine*, the iron-grated heat register. I sighed, unsure what to take. Finally I pointed to the painting and asked, "Is this one okay?"

Mom nodded. I took it down and wiped it clean, then handed it to Levi as he walked by with an armful of TV cable. I turned to the window and took the curtains down. Mom shooed a fly from the edge of the cake pan. I watched her finger the pink-flowered plates with knobby hands. Old hands. I ran my fingers through my hair.

Fred and Levi appeared in the doorway. Their laughter and good-natured jests echoed through the now-empty house. Levi said, "Trailer's full. We're gonna take off."

Mom stood up and shuffled into the living room, looking at the pile of discard. The rust-and-gold couch pillows, pieced from my sister Lila's bridesmaid dresses, were thrown carelessly on top. Underneath them was a crocheted afghan with a D-hanging-C brand stitched into the design—a gift from a family friend. These things covered chipped china, refrigerator magnets, mismatched buckets, a clock, linen napkins somewhat stained but neatly pressed, empty business folders, dried bouquets, a canister set, a silver-colored tray with embossed pineapples on it.

"No one wanted the grinder?"

"Well, Mom," I said gently, "I think I already have one. But, come to think of it, I should probably keep an extra around, just in case." I picked it out of the pile. "There are so many things we could use and that are really lovely, but we just don't have room for *all* of them."

Mom nodded. "The silver tray was my wedding gift."

"Oh, then of course we should keep that. I didn't know." I picked it out of the pile. "We can take anything else you want, Mom."

Mom looked over the pile again, then turned and walked back into the kitchen. I followed. Little rims of coal-furnace smoke outlined pale rectangles on the walls. Mom sat heavily in a chair and waited to serve her chocolate cake with the little stack of pink-flowered plates. Her daughters-in-law walked past her, empty-handed now, ready to leave.

"I gotta run, Granny. Gotta take the kids to practice," one said. "We'll drop by when you're settled."

Mom looked brighter at that point than she had all day as she said, "Take a piece of cake for them." She reached for the cake knife and a plate.

"Oh—no time. I'll take a rain check. We'll be sure and visit, Granny." And she was gone.

"I have to go too, Granny," another said. "I have to meet the vet at noon—couldn't reschedule. Sorry. We sure appreciate all the stuff."

"Let me get you a piece of cake," Mom said.

"Oh, no—I don't eat dessert. Maybe next time."

The family was gone. I heard the trailer pull out of the driveway. Refrigerator doors stood ajar. Cupboards were bare. Plastic twist ties and toothpicks were strewn in a corner. The wastebasket overflowed, and green garbage bags stood beside it. The kitchen drawers were pulled out, empty. The house was cold now with the damp spring draft of open doors. Mom still showed no emotion. I'm not sure what I expected.

It was just the two of us. Was I the mother now? Was she? I glanced around at my childhood home. My eyes threatened to tear. Why was *I* sad? Maybe because it seemed so final. I quickly stepped outside on the pretense of having to empty still-green pots of house-plants over the back fence. I crossed the yard and looked back at the house with its curtainless windows, and paused, pots in hand. Through the dining room pane I could see Mom, sitting by the chocolate cake with the stack of pink-flowered plates beside it, waiting for her children to stop their busy lives and eat a bite of cake.

Moving day, difficult, odd, and momentous as it was, came and went. But the changes had just begun. We settled Mom into her new room. Mom left a lot behind, and change wasn't easy for her. She missed the home place, the home routine. She wanted to bring a house dog but I think my husband's exact words were, "Over my dead body." She now puts up with my teenagers' noisy parties until midnight. My house isn't as clean and orderly as hers was—and absolutely *nothing* in my house is labeled and organized as it should be. Many of our meals are still eaten on the run to ball games, and our life is still fairly chaotic. Sometimes I wonder if she wishes for less busyness, more order and calm, or at least more quiet.

I made a few difficult changes as well. I now have an appliance mishmash and bowls of nuts to crack on my once-clear countertop, stinky rye bread in the breadbox, and green olives and odd bags of figs and dates in my fridge. Who in their right mind likes green olives? At least twice a month one of my children opens the fridge and says, "What *is* that?" Sure enough, there will be some new strange food there that Granny has picked up.

I also shopped for a cane, which certainly felt odd. Sometimes at two o'clock in the morning the sound of the microwave running wakes me up as she pops herself a bag of popcorn on a sleepless night. I also wake up occasionally to fresh-baked chocolate cake or popcorn balls or cinnamon rolls—at five o'clock in the morning. Or four or five loads of freshly folded laundry. Or a dozen still-warm ironed shirts. It's like waking up to Christmas. Because of Mom I took a mining class I wouldn't have otherwise taken. I pushed and pushed for a henhouse that I might not have without her. I'm a better gardener because she's here to encourage me and go through the headache of scouring all the seed catalogs and stores for the best deals. And flowers—I would have given up on flowers a long time ago if Mom didn't find such joy in planting them.

Our conversations of late go something like this, "Lynn, will you unpack the groceries?"

"Sure. Where do you want me to put this quart of honey? Wait, I know—next to the other three quarts you bought last month but forgot you had?" Then we laugh, and I know popcorn balls will show up very soon.

It's taken awhile, but I think we've made room for each other. Change has a way of doing that, you know—making us better individuals, if we let it. There is an alternative. We can resist it by kicking, screaming, and knocking our heads together, but that really only gets us very sore legs, very hoarse voices, and very bruised heads. I prefer popcorn balls.

Gentle Madness

If the premise is true that you need exercise to rid your muscles of toxins, then wouldn't it also hold true that you occasionally need to purge your mind of toxins as well? I have junk running around inside my head that is occupying perfectly good brain space. Thus, I purge with gardening.

The most wonderful thing about gardening is that it can be done at 6:30 A.M. in your pajamas. Nobody else is up and outside then, so nobody cares. The purging happens just between me and the beetles. Only at 6:30 A.M. can I come up with a good resignation letter for my employer—one that will bring tears to his eyes. I can come up with an amazing conference presentation. I can also wonder whether that crop duster who flies overhead at 6:30 A.M. every morning is in his pajamas too. (I ask you, who wants to carry *that* around in their brain?) Or how about those people who sit across from you at the Fourth of July parade? Don't you wonder what their life is like? What color their living room drapes are? What they're having for supper? Who yelled at whom last night? What they do on vacation? Where they'll go to watch fireworks? See, this brain-toxin thing just gets way out of hand. That's why I have to garden and detox.

If I don't dejunk my brain, then it just builds up and turns into what I think of as ugly tattoos. That's my theory—you either garden or you tattoo. I saw a man the other day with tattoos on his arm of—get this—locusts! You just have to wonder how he picked that, don't you? Did he just look at pictures of tigers, roses, chains, yin-ey yang-ey stuff, see the locust, and think, "Now *that* speaks to me." Did he think, "Locusts, all right! Chicks really dig bugs." I'm just not sure what was going through his head at the time. Probably lots of alcohol.

The choice is clear then: it's gardening or locusts.

Of course, some of us have more brain cells that *need* dejunking than others. But see, now my brain cells are all unloaded on you, and while I can work on other stuff, you're still going to have to wonder whether that crop duster is up there in his pajamas—unless you garden, of course.

Besides that, if it weren't for gardening, I wouldn't have found that perfectly good piece of Easter candy in the plum tree. The chocolate in it had turned white from the frost, but it was still amazingly soft and chewy. No earwigs anywhere. No day can go too terribly wrong when you start it with a bonus piece of chocolate.

Peas taste best coming straight from the pod, and the best drink of water in the world comes from a garden hose. So my advice to you is to garden at 6:30 A.M. Provided, of course, that you wear pajamas.

Stupid Plumber

One day I crossed paths with a really stupid plumber. (When I was little my mom said we couldn't call anyone "stupid." I have refrained until now—now that it really, truly *fits* someone.) That summer I had opened up the hatch door to the crawl space under the house to throw in some mouse poison, assuming that if I could kill the mice when they first tried to enter my house, they'd be too sick to actually come in. (I know—*too much information*.) But when I threw in the bar of poison, I heard a distinct splashing PLOP. I was pretty sure *that* wasn't supposed to happen. So I got out my flashlight and peered as far back under the house as I could—without actually coming nose to nose with a black widow or brown recluse spider—and, sure enough, we had a small lake under the house. So I called a plumber.

The plumber pulled up in his handy-dandy little tool truck with the name of his plumbing company proudly lettered on the side door. A real professional. I stood on the lawn while he crawled under the house. He didn't crawl under there much farther than I did; he was gone maybe thirty seconds and came right back out. This was his professional opinion:

"Ma'am," (it's never good when they call you ma'am) "there's a *lot* of water under there."

I'm thinking, *Yeah. Caught that.*

"It looks like a pipe might be broke."

"Do ya *think* so?!" But I don't say that. Instead, I say, "So you can fix that, right?"

"Yeah," he drawls, "but I'm gonna get awfully wet . . ."

What am I supposed to say to that? I decided to go with, "Uh-huh. Probably."

I went back in the house to let him do the plumberly thing. About fifteen or twenty minutes later he came knocking on the door.

"Ma'am" (here we go again), "it's awfully wet down there."

(In my efforts to rationalize what I said over the next few minutes, I just want you to know, in my defense, that I am usually very nonconfrontational. I may think really sarcastic things to myself but I really try to tone it down when I speak.) I spoke slowly and deliberately, "Yes. It's wet. That's—why—I—called—*you*."

He grumbled a bit under his breath on his way back to his pickup, but I really didn't have any sympathy. I watched out the kitchen window as he went to his truck and pulled out some rubber wading pants and boots. I relaxed a bit. Obviously he'd done this before. He'd just been stalling. He probably just wanted a little sympathy. I scolded myself—surely I could have empathized a bit. He crawled back under the house with an armload of tools and this time he was gone for maybe thirty minutes. Then I watched from the window as he went back to his truck (soaked up to his armpits) and took off his waders. His clothes were dry underneath except for his shirt, which he changed. It didn't look like he'd suffered all that much. He switched into his regular boots and knocked on the door again. He was more talkative this time (which I'm sure he regretted later).

"It was *really* deep. There was water everywhere. My shirt was soaked."

I wasn't sure why he felt the need to tell me this, but his complaining dispersed what empathy I *might* have been trying to muster, and I couldn't bite my tongue any longer.

"Mister, you're a PLUMBER. Why did you decide to be a PLUMBER if you didn't want to work with WATER? That's what you're SUPPOSED to do. Did you think when you went to plumbing school that somehow there wouldn't be any WATER involved?"

He grumbled the whole time I wrote out his check.

Now, sometimes a mind can wander and recall the strangest things at the oddest times. Granted some minds are a little stranger than others, but last week I was in sacrament meeting, and among all the things I should have been thinking, guess which stupid plumber story popped up somewhere between the youth speaker (who, by the way, pronounced "capacity" as "cap-a-CITY" which was kind of cute), and "Beautiful Zion Built Above?" Yes, *my* favorite stupid plumber story.

Our next two speakers that sacrament meeting were our wonderful full-time missionaries, who spoke on missionary work. So my thoughts were jumping from the stupid plumber to missionary work and back again, as—periodically, at least—I tried to focus. And then, in a peculiar, quirky kind of way, suddenly the two topics became one.

The plumber was balking at water. How stupid is that? That's what he's been educated to do. That's what he chose to do. That's what he's prepared and paid to do. That's how he makes his livelihood. And yet, is it any more ridiculous than me, as a member of The Church of Jesus Christ of Latter-day Saints, balking at missionary work? Spreading the gospel? That very thing that is going to further my own eternal progression? The very thing I've chosen to commit to for the rest of my life? The thing that will sustain me through time and eternity?

I have the restored gospel. I have access to saving ordinances. I have been taught and schooled in this gospel from my youth and have received my own personal witness of its truth at my own choosing. But, like the plumber, I balk at the very thing I've been prepared and sent to do.

Who's feeling stupid now?

I Haven't Lived This Long for Nothing

The greatest use of life is to spend it for something that will outlast it.
—*William James*

I have learned perhaps a few last things. Henceforth and forever more:

I will not constantly worry about whether the clothes I'm wearing fit the occasion. I will not worry whether my pantyhose colors are fashionably correct, whether a forty-five-year-old woman should be seen in public in tennis shoes, whether my hair is too long for anyone not twenty or too short for anyone not sixty. Nobody else really cares what I wear or how I look—they're too busy fussing over themselves.

I will not stew over whether I'll ever get to see Washington D.C., or take a cruise, or skydive, or live in a house with automatic lawn sprinklers. Memories are made when a child climbs on your lap, you play a three-day game of monster Monopoly, you have the flat tire on the freeway in the carpool lane, and you teach a Primary class three years longer than you ever thought you could. They are not made in vacation destinations or automatic sprinklers.

I won't get upset over little things like having to park half a mile from the mall entrance. I did, after all, have a car to drive there in.

I won't get in a dither about how clean the house is before I invite friends over. They're called *friends* for a reason.

I won't have a tizzy on my birthday because I'm getting older. Older is good. Older is smarter. Older has more perspective. Older has better priorities. And older has more clout.

I won't squirm on the church pew on Mother's Day because of all the imperfections I have as a mother and all the insecurities I have as a woman, or because of all the imperfections my parents had. There is no hidden agenda, no subtle undercurrent. It's not a guilt-trip. It's just okay.

I won't get my lips in a pucker over the justice my enemies deserve. I will plead for mercy for myself instead.

I won't toss and turn over not getting the recognition I deserve or over not being able to cement-curb the flower beds in my landscaping. Fame and riches are shallow and unworthy friends. As Elder Boyd K. Packer said: "The choice is not between fame and obscurity, nor is the choice between wealth and poverty. The choice is between good and evil, and that is a very different issue indeed" (*New Era*, Aug. 1989).

I won't stay awake nights scheming of ways to get even. Revenge is a poor victory.

I won't writhe like a hooked fish worrying about tomorrow's problems. I've heard it said that worry is like a good rocking chair—it'll give you something to do, but it won't get you anywhere. Several years ago when the old refrigerator-turned-meat-smoker had a propane explosion, Fred and Homer were standing nearby and their hair caught fire. So when worries arise and threaten to sap my strength, I will remember—at least my hair isn't on fire.

I won't agonize over what a program or organization becomes after I've left its ranks of service. What matters is how I served when I was there.

I won't work up a lather over the fact that the crops didn't produce, the cow dried up, the fruit trees were picked clean by the birds, and the summer lamb died. If I've loved and done my best to raise a bumper crop of children, then I succeeded in all that really matters.

When I get a good thought to do something nice for someone, I won't ignore it and I won't delay. I wouldn't want the Lord to have to find another angel for the job.

Nobody can name the last five Nobel Prize winners, or the last ten Pulitzer Prize winners, or even the ten richest people in the world. But almost everybody can tell you which teacher put an arm around him and helped him through a bad time, or who taught her to appreciate her craft, who brought her flowers, and who helped him cry. I will remember that.

We Americans are so proud of the fact that we fought a war where husbands, brothers, and fathers died to defend the right to live and worship as desired. What a wasted effort it was, what blood lies on my hands, if I don't bother getting up on Sunday morning to attend worship and make use of these gifts.

I believe I can't quit the fight. To conquer does not always mean to subdue or vanquish; sometimes it just means I can't surrender even though I seem to be losing the battle. It's not always a win/lose situation. Sometimes the victory is just to have endured. And "endured" is an interesting word. Many years ago I went on a fifty-mile backpack trip. The first day I slung on a thirty-seven-pound pack and charged up the trail, anxious to look strong and fit and be first. I sprinted (at least the best you can sprint in a thirty-seven-pound pack). By the second morning when I rolled over in my sleeping bag groaning, I thought, *This hurts. Somebody just shoot me.* The third morning when I rolled over in my bedroll, now beyond pain, I thought, *Never mind—I'll shoot myself.* Well, backpacking is not a sprint, and neither is life or testimony; it's a marathon. We're in it for the long haul. I will just endure.

I believe our greatest strengths are our greatest weaknesses—and vice versa. Once I find something I'm really good at, it's time to analyze that very thing to discover how it also weakens me.

I believe support is wonderful—but a person succeeds first in their head and heart, all alone, like Christ in Gethsemane. Even though the disciples waited at the gate, He was ultimately alone—the test was solitary. Life is not always a team sport. I may have friends or all the love of a family, but in my life's race no one but me moves each of my tired legs after another. It's *my* chest that screams for air. So I have to build that inner strength and learn to trust it; I can endure much more than I give myself credit for.

I believe in family. Paul the Apostle speaks of the body being whole—and the head cannot look at the foot and say, "I have no need of thee," etc. It all contributes to the whole. Bodies sometimes get diseased or injured or crippled. This can severely limit what the body was intended for—but sick as the body may become, it is still the very best vessel to house our spirits. Weak as it may become, it is still the temple best equipped to further our eternal progression. Similarly, the family may be dysfunctional, it may be very sick indeed, but it is still the best institution that is intended to make us grow. It affords us the best opportunity to learn charity, faith, and hope. It is worth working for. It is worth saving. It is worth the harried holiday dinners. It is worth suffering through lectures by insufferably opinionated family members. It is worth suffering through humiliation for. It is worth fighting for. And the responsibility of mothers and fathers will never cease. We must work at improving family relationships forever.

I believe that all of us are children of God. Due to divine heritage and through no effort of our own, we have inherent worth that we may not even be able to feel or see, but that doesn't mean we don't have it. Perhaps our life's journey is to discover it. Perhaps it is just to have the faith that it is there. Trust me on this one.

And I will remember that we, as women, may all be at different times and at different seasons of understanding in our lives. We may, some of us, be single, some of us married, some divorced, some with many children and some with none or few, some old and some young—we all have different oars, but we're all paddling the same canoe.